This Yoga Journal belongs to:

. . . .

On this day of . . . . , I commit to the yoga lifestyle through the daily practice of yoga, meditation, self-inquiry, connecting with my essence, exploring my potential and aligning with my destiny.

Signed:

. . . .

Dailygreatness Yoga Journal: Your Masterplan for a Beautifully Conscious Life

Lyndelle Palmer-Clarke

Help us spread our transformational journals with your friends by:

Sharing your journal images using hashtag #dailygreatnessjournal on social media
or review the Dailygreatness Yoga Journal on our website or on Amazon and go in
our monthly draw to win a free copy!

To reorder your Dailygreatness Yoga Journal and browse all our other journals,
online courses and content, visit www.dailygreatnessjournal.com

Design: Viktoriya Nesheva
Editing: Megan Peterson Morrow
Printed in China

Dreaming Room Publishing
First Edition Dreaming Room 2013

Your body
is your temple.

✶ ✶ ✶

If you were an architect and were planning on building a beautiful temple, the first thing you would need is a solid and stable foundation to build from. The Dailygreatness Yoga Journal is your foundation for building a beautifully conscious life and brings together all aspects of body, mind and spirit.

The daily practice of yoga is designed to challenge your self-imposed limitations -- through reconnecting with your true essence. As you do, you'll begin to experience your purest consciousness and highest potential — the truth of who you really are. Anyone can practise yoga — no matter what your age, experience level or current physical state, yoga will meet you where you are and allow you to get to know and love your body, mind and spirit more intimately and completely.

The tools in this journal will guide you in reconnecting to that essence, allowing you to be more grounded, creative and conscious. Soon your life will take on a whole new feeling of effortlessness as you eliminate stress, fear and unconscious patterns and behaviours.

With a unique combination of an organiser, a goal planner, and daily tools for body and mind mastery, the Dailygreatness Yoga Journal is your friend and guide on your inward journey every day throughout the next year.

The Daily Pages will guide you to create conscious habits and cultivate a beautiful mind. The weekly and quarterly check-ins and planners keep you organised, committed and accountable to your yoga practice. The self-inquiry questions will lead you on a journey of self-discovery helping you to reveal, clarify and act on your true desires. You'll learn to become solution-focused, productive, and begin to live with more compassion, joy and peace. Each stage lays the foundation for achieving your goals, perfecting your yoga practice and reaching your potential.

Just like an eagle learning to fly, you will feel your boundaries expand and your potential grow sky-high with each new day. As you quest towards your potential, purifying your body and your mind, you'll begin to let go of all that holds you back, shine your light and create your beautifully conscious life.

This journal is dedicated to you -- for believing in your potential, your greatness and the awesomeness of who you really are, which is what yoga is all about.

Namaste,

Attuning to Your Inner Landscape

If you want to live in a better world, look within – it all begins with you! Each one of us creates the world that we live in, with every thought we think, every word we speak and every action we take. Our reality is completely of our own making, based on the perceptions and the filters through which we view life. Taking responsibility for ourselves and how we show up in the world every day is how we shape the world we live in. Through your yoga practice, you have an incredible opportunity to enhance both your life and the world as a whole.

The 8 Daily Steps I'm about to share with you are a perfect balance between doing (action) and being (connection). When your actions support your connection, you become the powerful co-creator of your reality. All action with no inner connection might keep you busy, but you'll be out of touch with your inner power and truth. All connection (meditating all day, for example) and no action will result in not fulfilling your potential. The perfect balance of both action and connection will weave magic in your life.

Each morning session is designed to connect you to your inner knowing and your higher self, and each evening self-inquiry session is designed for you to become conscious of your strengths, your challenges and where you can grow.

This may be unlike anything you've done in the past, but remember, genuine transformation comes from upgrading our thoughts, beliefs and behaviours. It is not only what you do on the yoga mat but how you take your yoga practice into the world that will make all the difference to the quality of your life.

When your inner and outer worlds are in sync, you'll begin to experience more balance and flow as a result. Even the smallest of upgrades can create huge shifts in your everyday life. Noticing these upgrades will inspire you to continue your inward journey, and by committing to your yoga practice and The 8 Daily Steps, you'll gain even more momentum and overcome resistance that may have held you back in the past. It's truly the journey of a lifetime!

Side note: You might have noticed I like to use enhance or upgrade instead of words like fix, improve or change. The idea is that we don't need to "fix" anything. Spiritual growth isn't about being perfect, it's about being conscious and revealing more of our true selves by letting go of what no longer serves us. We're all on an upward spiral towards becoming a more evolved version of ourselves, peeling back layers of conditioning and self-imposed limitations along the way. Upgrading your thoughts, beliefs and behaviours results in empowered thinking, clarity in decision-making, more productive actions and reaching your potential. So from now on, let's agree to use positive language when we talk about changing or improving anything.

What's Your Dharma?

Consider the idea that we all have an inner and an outer purpose. Our inner purpose is to grow, evolve and come to know our true potential. Our outer purpose is to use our talents to do our soul's work.

To put it another way, your life purpose is to enrich the world through your unique talents and gifts. When you do what you love and love what you do, while at the same time serving others, you're fulfilling your highest purpose. In Eastern philosophy, this is called dharma – your essential function or purpose in life. Soon you'll have a chance to craft your very own Purpose and Personal Mission Statements designed to help you fulfill your dharma over the next year combined with your yoga practice.

The Journey

Your first step to a beautifully conscious life is simply to make the decision. A decision from your heart is a force to be reckoned with, and is the power you need to point you in the direction of your truth. The next step is to go within to find out what you truly desire and begin to uncover your purpose by deciding what meaning your life will have.

The Dailygreatness Yoga Journal will help you make fresh new choices and discover what you truly desire through celebrating your achievements, identifying your values, awakening to your purpose, believing in your dreams and developing a plan for achieving your goals.

After carefully considering your deepest desires, inner longings and core values, you will then create your Conscious Life Blueprint.

Conscious Life Blueprint

Your Conscious Life Blueprint is your yearly master plan; your highest vision of what you'd like to consciously create over the coming year in all 8 areas of your life. It's a tool for getting clear about what you want, why you want it and for creating an action plan for making it happen. The key to this is the word "conscious." While we spend so much time racing around mindlessly, this process is all about paying attention to what we authentically desire, looking within and creating from the heart. Spend time going inward to really consider what it is you want to create before mapping out your Conscious Life Blueprint.

Side Note: All these instructions might seem a little overwhelming right now, but soon they will all make perfect sense. Just relax, enjoy and let the pages guide you.

Creating Goals with Soul

Goals are our dreams broken down into achievable actions with a deadline. They give our life meaning, a sense of purpose and fulfillment. When creating goals, you need to consider all the dimensions of your life: body, mind and spirit. Goals can be big or small, but most of all, they must be meaningful to you, or you won't have the drive to achieve them. We often look outside ourselves for what we think we want, but we need to consult our hearts rather than our heads to find what we authentically desire for our lives. Otherwise, down the track we may end up with a whole lot of "things" in life, while missing what we are really looking for – happiness and fulfillment. It's important to remember that it's not the achievement of your goals that matters so much but who you become while questing towards them.

As I've said before, all change starts within. To achieve and sustain your goals, a shift must first occur on the inside before you'll see the physical manifestation of it on the outside. When you expand your consciousness through yoga and self-awareness practices, even seemingly impossible goals can be achieved through aligning yourself with the infinite field of possibilities that already lies within you. When this inner transformation happens, the outer condition seems to transform itself almost effortlessly.

The secret to creating goals with soul is knowing why you want something. If you can't come up with a strong why, then you probably don't really want it. Your why comes from your core values and what's most important to you. If your goals aren't congruent with your values, you'll find yourself unconsciously sabotaging yourself – or you may achieve your goal, but you won't feel fulfilled.

When pursuing a big goal, it's natural to feel fear. Fear is there to warn us when we are moving into unknown territory. This is a good sign. All our goals and dreams live outside our comfort zone, and fear is just a signpost telling you that you're getting closer to your goal! When you work through your fear and persist, you will find the happiness and fulfillment, you are looking for.

Finally, remember, there's a big difference between desperation and determination. Attachment to your goals pushes them away, while non-attachment allows the perfect experience to unfold for your highest good. So have fun creating your goals with soul and then let go!

For a 6-step process on creating meaningful goals, see Appendix i.

Tip: Putting together a beautiful vision board can serve as a dynamic, visual reminder that will keep your Conscious Life Blueprint fresh in your mind each day.

Rituals, Habits & Magic

Forming a new habit takes time. To successfully integrate any new habit or practice into your daily routine, it's useful to create a ritual. Working with your journal and practising yoga at the same time every day will help you develop a great habit and daily ritual. Give yourself the best chance by putting your Dailygreatness Yoga Journal by your bed, near your yoga mat, in your kitchen or somewhere you will see it easily. Keeping it close by will help you follow through. Don't put it on your bookshelf and forget about it! Magic isn't just an accidental "abracadabra," rather it happens when you stay committed, focused and follow through on your promises.

Exercise: Write a letter to your future self, right now. Describe clearly what you want to achieve within one year. At the end of the year, once you have completed the journal, you will read the letter and see how much you've grown and what you've accomplished. Go write it now, seal it in an envelope, write the date on the outside and mark your diary to read it in one year.

Self-Mastery & the Dark Side

Self-inquiry is your entry point into self-mastery and true personal transformation. The tools and self-inquiry questions throughout the Dailygreatness Yoga Journal are designed to help you become more conscious and positive, but focusing only on the positive, and failing to acknowledge your fears, limiting beliefs or undeveloped aspects limits your ability to achieve your true potential.

These unconscious aspects lie hidden in our subconscious mind until something triggers them to pop up and sabotage our best intentions. Persistent and committed effort is required if we are to use our dark side as a steppingstone into a better life, free from fear, reactivity and false beliefs.

Naturally, through your yoga practice and by working through the journal, you will begin to open up in ways that may sometimes make you feel wonderful, and at other times make you feel uncomfortable and even emotional. This is completely normal. Old habits die hard, and as we confront our fears, our unconscious habits and patterns often rise to the surface, so we can finally face them consciously before letting them go.

Be brave, embrace your dark side for the incredible lessons and gifts it has for you, and keep moving forward.

Who are Your Five Closest Friends?

Surrounding yourself with people who understand your new lifestyle choices and who support you in positive ways is essential once you've made the decision to live a conscious life. Your environment and external influences play a huge role in your ability to live consciously and reach your potential. Who are the five people who will support you every step of the way? Believe in you? And always have your back? Keep these friends close.

If you are not currently surrounded by people who have goals, dreams and values similar to yours, then find a community of people who do. In short, hang out with and learn from people who inspire you, uplift you, empower you and support you.

Getting Lost

It's easy to start strong on a new adventure, but harder to stay inspired after the initial excitement. You'll probably hit a few dips and bumps with your practice, and even miss a few days here and there, so be prepared for some backsliding.

If you do, don't worry! It's okay! This is not about being perfect, it's about being conscious of the choices you make so you can make better choices next time. Simply acknowledge any issues that come up and ask yourself a few questions, like:

What was the trigger that knocked me off track?
Am I still inspired by my goals?
What fears are holding me back?
Why am I procrastinating?
What am I choosing to focus on?
What do I need to let go of?
What don't I want, and what would I prefer?
What addictions do I need to acknowledge and let go of?
How can I be more present and live more consciously?
How can I change my yoga routine to make it more fun?

Use your answers to empower yourself to make adjustments to your plans and then recommit to your vision and your daily practice.

The 8 Daily Steps:
Your Foundation to a Beautifully Conscious Life

The 8 Daily Steps are short, focused sessions
in the morning and evening designed to;
align you with your intentions, allow you to
think more creatively, train your mind to focus on
gratitude and open you up to being fully conscious
and aware in all your day to day interactions. The gift
of a morning and evening practice will create huge shifts
in the quality and productiveness of your days.

How you choose to use the journal, and how much time you
spend on each step is entirely up to you. I recommend a minimum
of 30 minutes for the morning session, plus 25 minutes of yoga
and a minimum of 15 minutes for the evening self-inquiry questions.
Though I recommend following this morning and evening framework,
feel free to refer to your journal any time you need a little extra inspiration
or a boost to your spirit!

It can be overwhelming when looking at the big picture, but think of your daily
practice as the basis for reinventing yourself one thought, one pose, one intention,
one day at a time. In the beginning, you may want to go slowly by incorporating a
new step every few days until you get into the swing of all 8 Daily Steps.

At first, it may seem like nothing is happening and that the journal is not working. Continue
on, push through your resistance and soon you'll have breakthroughs in your productivity,
creativity, self-belief, determination, health and your overall attitude.

1. Meditation

Practising meditation in the morning is a powerful way to deepen your connection with spirit, build your character, raise your consciousness and connect to your true essence. Meditation helps you quiet the mind so you can open up to your gifts of intuition and creativity, and it is achieved through stillness and conscious breathing. Meditation doesn't need to be complicated: Simply sit in a comfortable position, allow yourself to become relaxed, centered and present, and focus on your breath. Whenever your mind wanders off (and it will!), just bring it right back to your next breath. Start with just 10 to 15 minutes twice a day and over time you'll find you can sit for longer periods. Tip: Make 25 minutes your goal; something magical happens at the 25-minute mark. See appendix ii for instructions on basic meditation technique.

2. Yoga

Yoga is designed to awaken you to your true nature and to the realisation that you truly are a magnificent spiritual being with unlimited potential. Your body is your temple and as you perfect your yoga practice and purify your body and mind you will begin to experience more joy, peace and awareness. A good daily yoga practice will help you slow down so you can tune in to your inner voice and open up to your full potential. Yoga is a powerful way to balance the right and left hemispheres of the brain, release blockages in the chakras and energy centers, reduce stress, and maintain and ground the energy within your body. Your energy is your most valuable resource; with vital energy you can achieve all your goals. The more energy you have, the more productive you will be. Start your day with deep conscious breathing through the nose followed by your favourite sequence of yoga poses. Create a dynamic daily yoga routine at home or catch a class at your local yoga studio or even online and then record your practice on the daily pages. As you challenge yourself to find your edge you'll begin to appreciate your greatness and the awesome potential that lies within you.

3. Heart-Centered Gratitude

Starting your day in a state of gratitude is a powerful way to open you up for being in flow with the universe. Using the daily gratitude list, write down everything that you are grateful for each day. It may be as simple as blue skies, the clothes you're wearing, the energy you have to practise yoga, books for new knowledge or a friendship you treasure. Be grateful for things that are still to come, like new possibilities, opportunities and awakenings. Remember, whatever you focus on, you will attract more of.

4. Inspired Action

Inspired Action is the key to tapping your inner genius and for living with enthusiasm, vitality and flow. When your actions are inspired, they have power and focus. With inspiration, your fear decreases and your actions become almost effortless. Instead of doing what you "have to do," these actions are things you "love to do." It could be a creative project, an income-producing activity that you enjoy, a hobby or anything that lights you up and makes you feel good. It's about following your bliss! Each day you will choose your top 3 Inspired Actions. These are meant to move you closer to your overall master plan and vision for the year. As you use the Dailygreatness Yoga Journal and open up to your inner guidance, be alert to hunches, ideas and synchronicities that show up and guide you in certain directions or give you flashes of inspiration and insight. When you clearly know what you want and why you want it, the inspiration will be there to guide you.

Tip: After you've meditated, take some time to ask your inner genius what the best actions are to take that day and then contemplate and take action on what comes up. Here are some suggestions:

What right action should I take today?
What do I need to know today?
What would I love to do today?
What inspires me today?
What action will move me closer to my goals today?

5. Intentions

Clearly stating your intentions declares to both yourself and the universe how you intend to co-create your days. Saying your intentions aloud aligns your head and your heart and creates a powerful platform from which to launch your days. Your intention is your point of focus, your mindset, and what you intend to be, do or have in any given moment. Intention is your underlying motivation and, more than anything else, is responsible for the results you get in life. Every positive thought attracts, every negative thought repels and each new day is a new opportunity to create a beautifully conscious life.

Consciously choosing your intentions each day will direct your focus and energy so that you stay centered, no matter what is happening around you. An intention can be a word, a personal value or an affirmation starting with "I AM" that reminds and guides you to your highest truth. For example: I AM love, I AM aware, I AM opening to my potential.

Through our intentions, we become the masters of our own energy, consciously choosing our frequency and our emotional state, rather than mindlessly reacting to the world around us. Intention includes being conscious in our communication and the energy we put behind the words we write and speak to ourselves and to others.

It's important to feel your intention throughout your body as you state it aloud. This will anchor the energy of the intention into your body's cellular memory, so choose your intentions carefully, since they will become your reality.

6. Inspiration

A complement to Inspired Actions, inspiration is essential to keep your inner flame burning, to fuel your purpose and to keep your energy elevated so you can continually expand and move towards your potential. Stay inspired each day by reading your purpose statement out loud, reflecting on a daily quote, listening to music that inspires and uplifts you, or, of course, get inspired on your yoga mat! Consider reading stories of people who are making a difference in the world; use their courage to inspire you to shine your light and stay on track towards your purpose and goals. However you choose to stay inspired, being in a positive state of mind opens you up to greater possibilities for your

life, and when you're inspired you inspire others to shine their light also.

7. Soul Space

Give your soul some space to breathe. Soul Space is just that: A space to journal your thoughts, your feelings, your ideas, your dreams, your insights. Increasing your self-awareness also means becoming conscious of your dream state. Dreams hold powerful messages and help us to live more consciously in our daily lives. Start by writing down your dreams as soon as you wake up. The more you do this, the more you will remember them.

Tip: If you need more space for writing and recording your dreams, ideas and other inspirations, you might want to use a separate blank journal.

8. Self-Inquiry Power Questions

Asking questions is a powerful process that activates your internal search engine to come up with solutions and new possibilities. It's not about trying to achieve a certain desirable state or stopping your less desirable emotions. It's much simpler! It's about exploring how you feel in the present moment and relaxing into this expanded awareness while being alive, awake and conscious of the state you're in. Through self-inquiry, you begin discovering new ways to live a more conscious, empowered and inspired life. The better your questions, the better your answers will be. Throughout the journal, you'll find many self-inquiry questions, but don't limit yourself to these. Challenge yourself to ask questions that will trigger the answers you're looking for. Each evening take 15 minutes to answer the evening Self-Inquiry Questions to debrief and evaluate your day.

Tip: In the evening, spend time planning your day ahead using the Daily Pages, consider your intentions for tomorrow, and contemplate and plan your top 3 Inspired Actions. This will clear your mind for a good night's sleep and you'll have a clear vision of your day ahead so you can use your time purposefully from the moment your feet hit the floor.

The Check-Ins

Weekly Check-In and Planner

Every Sunday during your Weekly Check-In, you'll have the opportunity to reflect back over the past week, and decide what's working and what isn't by bringing these areas into your conscious awareness and resetting your focus for the next week.

You'll then plan your coming week to get a clear view of your goals, projects and plans with the Weekly Planner. This is also a good time to review your Conscious Life Blueprint, your Purpose Statement and your goals to keep yourself moving towards them.

90-Day Check-In & Planner

Every quarter, you'll do a 90-Day Check-In where you'll answer a series of questions designed to help you get a high-level view on where you are in life. The questions will help you consciously identify areas that you'd like to upgrade and, even better, to celebrate your progress! You'll then reset your focus and plan your next 90 days using the 90-Day Planner.

The Weekly and 90-Day Check-Ins are designed to help you stay committed, conscious and curious. They highlight areas of your life that need attention by bringing them into your conscious awareness and help you upgrade disempowering habits and transform them to new empowering thoughts, actions and behaviours.

Yearly Review

At the end of the journal, you will have a Yearly Review, giving you a chance to reflect on and celebrate your achievements, learn from your challenges and consolidate your thoughts, before launching into another beautifully conscious year.

Tip: Although the journal is filled with useful planners to help you prepare and take action towards your dreams, it's important not to forget about your yoga practice and your inner work. Resist using the journal solely as a diary or planner, since all 8 Daily Steps are essential to achieve a conscious, successful and purposeful year.

Is what you are doing today getting you where you want to be tomorrow?

★ ★ ★ ★ ★ ★

Self-Inquiry Power Questions:

Health & Body

What is one thing I can do every day to take good care of my body?
Do I eat too much or too little for a strong, healthy body?
What can I do to create more energy in my life?
What do I need to STOP doing?
What do I need to START doing?
What big fitness goal could I set for myself in the next 12 months?
Do I drink enough water?
How can I focus my diet on fresh healthy foods that bring more vitality to my life?
What does my body need right now?
What beliefs do I hold that prevent me from having the health/fitness/body I want?

Emotional, Spiritual & Personal Growth

How can I let go of limiting beliefs and attitudes?
What kind of person do I aspire to be?
What are my beliefs about the nature of reality, God and why I am here?
Who am I?
How can I be more authentic, more true to myself?
What baggage do I have that holds me back?
Do I complain? Am I generally positive or negative?
What stops me from being authentic and true to my wants and desires?
What do I stand for?
What fears do I have about the future?
How can I trust life more?
Who do I need to forgive? Have I forgiven myself?
Do I listen to my heart?
What do I need to let go of to move forward?
What is no longer acceptable in my life?
What qualities do I wish to develop?
What is my intuition telling me about my purpose?

Intimate Relationships

What are three things that I most appreciate about my partner?
Do I communicate consciously?
How can I bring more love into my relationships?
What are our relationship goals?
How can I be more open-minded and accepting of my partner?
What are my partner's dreams?
When do we have the most fun together?
Does my partner fulfill my needs and do I fulfill his/hers?

Social and Fun

How can I have more fun?
What new hobby or sport could I start?
What do I love to do? What makes me happy?
What would I love to experience or create, if I had no excuses?
What club or group could I join to be more social?
What's missing in my life?
What would I do if no one was looking?

Family and Friends

How can I give more value to those around me?
What is one thing I can do to improve my relationship with my family?
How can I listen more to those in my life?
Where could I be less judgmental?
How can I expand my network and friendships?
Do I have a relationship that needs mending?
How can I surround myself with the best people?
How can I be a better father/mother/sister/brother/daughter/son?
How can I be a better friend?
Who do I need to set healthy boundaries with?

Work and Career

What do I want to do with the rest of my life?
What is my definition of success?
What is my unique message and contribution?
What have I struggled with in the past?
How can I better handle obstacles and disappointments?
Am I willing to take measured risks to pursue my dreams?
What lies in the deepest part of my heart still to be expressed?
How can I shine my light and in turn inspire others to shine their light?
How can I be a better leader?
What is the best and highest use of my talents?
How can I be more creative?
What new skills would I like to develop?
How can I be a better team player?
What course would I love to take?

Money and Finances

Is making money or making a difference more important?
Is it possible to do both?
How can I open myself to abundance and receiving more money in my life?
What decisions do I need to make that I have been putting off?
Who are my professional advisors?
What are my beliefs about money?
Which old beliefs about money do I need to replace with new ones?
Do I believe I deserve money?
What is one idea that I have not yet acted on that could be a successful venture?
Where and how do I sabotage my finances?
How can I get more educated on money and finances?
Do I ask enough questions when it comes to my money, finances and investments?

Community & Giving

How can I take my yoga practice off the mat and into the world?
Where can I give more of my time, money or support?
How can I be a leader in my community?
What small upgrades can I make to my lifestyle that will positively impact the world?
What do I feel passionate about and want to support more openly?
What big community goal could I set for the next 12 months that would greatly help others?
How can I show my concern or compassion for others?
Who could be my mentor or who could I mentor?

Forgiveness Sets You Free

Your leaping off point starts with forgiveness. Is there anyone or anything you need to forgive in order to move forward with your life? It could be a person, an event, a failed business, a lost dream, a broken relationship. How about some self-forgiveness?

Anything you've invested your energy in uses up your precious life force. Now is the time to forgive, and begin to let it go. A great way to do that is to write yourself or someone else a letter that you never post. Others don't need to know that you're forgiving them for this to be effective. Forgiveness happens inside you. The most important thing is to stop holding the pain in your mind and in your body. Use this exercise to free up your energy and reclaim your power.

Celebrate Your Life

Sometimes we need to remember how great we already are. Years go by, and we lose track of our achievements and how much we've grown and become. We focus on our "failures" and the negative experiences overshadow the highlights. It's time now to be honest with yourself and see your life with a renewed perspective. Start with your childhood and do a full inventory, consolidating your life achievements to date, no matter how small they might seem now. Keep writing until you have listed them all up through today. Refer to this page whenever you want to feel good about yourself, and grateful for all that life has given you. Every 90 days come back and update this page with your latest and greatest achievements.

What Really Matters to You?

Your values are your compass—they point you towards what really matters to you and are your underlying motivation for all your choices in life. Identifying your values is an important step in becoming congruent. When your actions are congruent with your values, you will easily achieve your goals, align with your purpose and reach your potential. When all of these are aligned, you are in flow and when you're in flow, magic happens. A great question to ask yourself on a regular basis is, "What really, truly matters to you?" Start by identifying your core values from the list below, then circle the top five values that resonate with you the most. If none of these resonate, write your own in the space below.

Adventure	Fulfillment	Kindness	Self-reliance
Balance	Forgiveness	Knowledge	Service
Confidence	Fun	Love	Spirituality
Control	God	Lifestyle	Strength
Creativity	Growth	Marriage	Success
Discipline	Happiness	Peace of mind	Truth
Education	Health	Power	Unity
Faith	Hope	Progress	Wealth
Family	Honesty	Reason	Wisdom
Financial Security	Humour	Respect	
Friends	Independence	Security	
Freedom	Integrity	Self-expression	

What matters to me most is: ....

....

....

....

....

....

....

....

....

....

....

....

....

....

Dreaming Is Divine

Here's your opportunity to let go of fear, let your imagination run wild and dare to dream big. Your dreams are meant to excite you! When you have a big dream, one that you're excited to achieve, it gives you the fuel and motivation to continue your daily yoga practice as you quest towards your dreams. So, ask yourself:

What is really possible? ....

....

....

....

....

....................What do I feel passionate about? ....

....

....

....

....What have I always wished for in my life? ....

....

....

....

....................What is deep within my heart, waiting to be expressed? ....

....

....

....

.... What were

my childhood dreams and which ones still resonate? ....

....

....

....

............................What would I love to be, do or have?...

....

....

....

.... If money or time wasn't an

issue and I knew I couldn't fail, what would I do? ....

....

....

....

....

What Do You Desire?

Goals are simply dreams with a deadline. When creating goals, be as specific as possible and set a deadline for each goal. Use these questions to get clear on what you truly desire to have or who you aspire to be.

What do I want?
Why do I want it?
How will I make it happen?
What are the actions I need to take?
When will I have it?
Who do I need to be to achieve my goals?
Which fears and limiting beliefs do I need to let go of to reach this goal?

....
....
....
....
....
....
....
....
....
....
....
....
....
....
....
....
....
....
....
....
....
....
....
....
....
....
....

★ ★ ★

You
are enough.
You have enough.
There is nothing
outside of you that
will make you happier.
When you look
inside, you realise
everything you
need is already
within
you.

★ ★ ★

Purpose Statement

Your Purpose Statement is a clear, concise statement summing up your life purpose, and the reasons you do what you do. It should inspire and motivate you to reach for your potential each day, and becomes the driving force behind all your choices, intentions and actions.

Here are a few questions to help uncover your purpose:

Who am I and why am I here?
What legacy do I want to leave?
What gifts and talents do I wish to share with the world?
What have I learnt in my life that I can pass on to others?
What is my message?
What makes me come alive?
What does life want from me?
What is it that wants to be expressed through me?

An example of a Purpose Statement would be: "To awaken to my potential and help others awaken to theirs."

Take some time to craft your Purpose Statement below.

....
....
....
....
....
....
....
....
....
....
....
....
....
....
....
....
....
....
....
....

My Personal Mission Statement

Your Personal Mission Statement is a paragraph that clearly states how you will achieve your purpose. It can include qualities and values that you will embody and what your life, work and contributions are about.

Both your Personal Mission Statement and Your Purpose Statement will change and evolve as you do, so don't worry too much about getting it perfect right away. Instead, let both of these statements be fluid. As you read and review your statements on a regular basis, you will find yourself embodying the thoughts and behaviours of your future self. As you become increasingly like your ideal self, you'll naturally begin to shine your light and bring your message and purpose into the world.

An example of a Personal Mission Statement might be: "Through my unique gifts and talents as a teacher, I help others courageously explore, creatively express, and consciously embrace our extraordinary human journey."

Of course, it could be much simpler or more complex than this.

Take some time to craft a Personal Mission Statement that expresses what you wish to share with the world and what you want to realize within yourself.

My Conscious Life Blueprint

WHAT is my specific goal & outcome? What do I want? What would I LOVE to have?

WHY do I want it? This is my purpose and fuel for achieving it. How will this goal benefit my life or how will it affect my life, if I don't achieve it?

Add to Yearly & 90 Day Planner	Use as part of your Mission & Purpose Statement
Health & Body	
Emotional, Spiritual & Personal Growth	
Intimate Relationship	
Social & Fun	
Family & Friends	
Work & Career	
Money & Finances	
Community & Giving	

WHO do I need to be?
What mindset do I need in order
to achieve this goal?

HOW am I going to make it happen?
These are the specific projects,
actions and steps broken down as part
of my daily and weekly actions.

WHEN will I achieve it?
This is my timeframe for making it happen.

WHICH barriers/fears/limitations
do I need to overcome to
achieve this goal?

Watch your thoughts; they become words. Watch your words; they become actions. Watch your actions; they become habits. Watch your habits; they become character. Watch your character; for it becomes your destiny.

★ ★ ★

Lao Tzu

Yearly Planner

January >
week

1

2

3

4

February >
week

1

2

3

4

March >
week

1

2

3

4

April >
week

1

2

3

4

May >
week

1

2

3

4

June >
week

1

2

3

4

July >
week

1

2

3

4

October >
week

1

2

3

4

August >
week

1

2

3

4

November >
week

1

2

3

4

September >
week

1

2

3

4

December
week

1

2

3

4

Be
true to
yourself
by being true
to this moment.

* * *

A Beautifully Conscious Life

Dedication

Flexibility

Release

Flow

Discipline

Surrender

Strength

Integrity

Yoga

Presence

Stamina

Breath

Self-Inquiry

Contemplation

Meditation

Balance

Spirit

Concentration

Essence

90 day planner

Goal:

Target date:

Actions to complete this goal:

1.

2.

3.

4.

Why I'd love to achieve this goal:

How will I feel when I've reached this goal?

Goal:

Target date:

Actions to complete this goal:

1.

2.

3.

4.

Why I'd love to achieve this goal:

How will I feel when I've reached this goal?

Goal:

Target date:

Actions to complete this goal:

1.

2.

3.

4.

Why I'd love to achieve this goal:

How will I feel when I've reached this goal?

Goal:

Target date:

Actions to complete this goal:

1.

2.

3.

4.

Why I'd love to achieve this goal:

How will I feel when I've reached this goal?

Month:

Month:

date:

soul space

My Yoga Practice

Today I am so **grateful** for...

	Meditation		Inspiration
	Yoga Practice		....

My top 3 **inspired actions** for today are...

6.00
7.00

My **intentions** for today are...

I AM

I AM

I AM

8.00
9.00

What did I notice about my **yoga** practice today?

10.00
11.00
12.00

What did I **learn** today?

13.00
14.00

After today, what **behaviour** do I want to upgrade?

15.00
16.00
17.00

What **strengths** did I use today?

18.00
19.00

date:

My Appreciation & gratitude list

Meditation   Inspiration

Yoga Practice   . . . .

6.00

7.00

Today, I am most inspired to do...

8.00

The mindset I wish to create today is...

I AM

I AM

9.00

I AM

10.00

What did I enjoy about today?

11.00

12.00

What challenged me today that I can learn from?

13.00

14.00

What new yoga pose would I like to perfect?

15.00

16.00

17.00

What did I do really well today?

18.00

19.00

date:

My Yoga Practice

The things I am **grateful** for in my life are...

Today, I would **love** to do:

Today **i am focusing** on being...

I AM

I AM

I AM

What did I notice about my **thoughts** today?

What could I have handled **differently** today?

How can I open to **new** possibilities?

What am I **proud** of that came about today?

Meditation   Inspiration

Yoga Practice   ....

I AM
happy,
healthy &
connected

6.00

7.00

8.00

9.00

10.00

11.00

12.00

13.00

14.00

15.00

16.00

17.00

18.00

19.00

dream space

date:

gratitude is Wisdom...

Meditation   Inspiration

Yoga Practice   ....

Today, I feel **inspired** to do...

6.00

7.00

I create my day with my **thoughts**, therefore...

8.00

I AM

I AM

9.00

I AM

10.00

What did I **love** about my yoga practice today?

11.00

12.00

In what ways would I like to **grow**?

13.00

14.00

What would I like to **let go** of?

15.00

16.00

17.00

What was my underlying **motivation** today?

18.00

19.00

date:

soul space

When I am **grateful** I open up to more...

What would I do **today**, if it was my last?

Today...
I AM
I AM
I AM

What was **interesting** about today?

What am I not **seeing**?

What ideas would I like to **upgrade**?

When was I completely in the **moment** today?

My Yoga Practice

Meditation		Inspiration	
Yoga Practice		....	

6.00

7.00

8.00

9.00

10.00

11.00

12.00

13.00

14.00

15.00

16.00

17.00

18.00

19.00

My Yoga Practice

heart space

date:

☐ Meditation   ☐ Inspiration

☐ Yoga Practice   ☐ ....

6.00

7.00

8.00

9.00

10.00

11.00

12.00

13.00

14.00

15.00

16.00

17.00

18.00

19.00

Today, I give **thanks** for...

My **inspired** actions for today are...

Today I **honour** how I feel and...

I AM

I AM

I AM

What was today's **lesson**?

How can I create a more **challenging** yoga practice?

What do I **know** that I'm not admitting?

What **strengths** did I use today?

weekly check - in

	09.00	13.00	17.00
	10.00	14.00	18.00
	11.00	15.00	19.00
	12.00	16.00	20.00

What have I achieved this week?

What's working with my practice and why is it working?

What's not working and what am I willing to do to upgrade it?

What is one thing I can do this week that will create the biggest results in my life?

What do I need to make a decision about?

How can I be more authentic?

What beliefs are holding me back and how can I upgrade them?

How can I open my chakras for more connection to my source?

Review Conscious Life Blueprint

Review Purpose Statement

Update 90-Day Planner

Add Actions to Weekly Planner

Plan Your Week

Old Habit >

New Habit >

New Actions >

New Affirmation/Mantra/Yoga Pose

weekly planner

4 Major Goals I'm Focused On This Week:			
1	**2**	**3**	**4**

Projects & Appointments For This Week	Target date	Actions & Yoga Practice For This Week	Target date
monday			
tuesday			
wednesday			
thursday			
friday			
saturday			
sunday			

date:

creative space

What I **love** about my work is...

Today I am inspired to take these **actions**:

I have a **beautiful** mind and...

I AM

I AM

I AM

What did I **learn** on the yoga mat today?

How was my **mindset** today?

What new **habit** do I want to adopt into my life?

Where am I at this very moment?

Meditation   Inspiration

Yoga Practice   ....

6.00

7.00

8.00

9.00

10.00

11.00

12.00

13.00

14.00

15.00

16.00

17.00

18.00

19.00

dream space

date:

I am so grateful for **simple** things like...

Meditation   Inspiration

Yoga Practice   ....

6.00

7.00

What is the best course of **action** to take today?

8.00

9.00

Today I **am** creative and...

I AM

I AM

I AM

10.00

Who AM I?

11.00

12.00

What am I supposed to do right **now**?

13.00

14.00

15.00

What new **mindset** do I want to adopt into my life?

16.00

17.00

How did my **yoga** practice feel today?

18.00

19.00

date:

soul space

 My Yoga Practice

Today I am so **grateful** for...

My top 3 **inspired actions** for today are...

My **intentions** for today are...

I AM

I AM

I AM

What did I notice about my **yoga** practice today?

What did I **learn** today?

After today, what **behaviour** do I want to upgrade?

What **strengths** did I use today?

Meditation   Inspiration

Yoga Practice   ....

6.00

7.00

8.00

9.00

10.00

11.00

12.00

13.00

14.00

15.00

16.00

17.00

18.00

19.00

heart space

date:

My Appreciation & gratitude list

Meditation   Inspiration

Yoga Practice   ....

6.00

7.00

Today, I am most inspired to do...

8.00

The mindset I wish to create today is...

I AM

I AM

9.00

I AM

10.00

What did I enjoy about today?

11.00

12.00

What challenged me today that I can learn from?

13.00

14.00

I AM awakening to my potential

15.00

What new yoga pose would I like to perfect?

16.00

17.00

What did I do really well today?

18.00

19.00

date:

creative space

My Yoga Practice

The things I am **grateful** for in my life are...

Today, I would **love** to do:

Today **i am focusing** on being...

I AM

I AM

I AM

What did I notice about my **thoughts** today?

What could I have handled **differently** today?

How can I open to **new** possibilities?

What am I **proud** of that came about today?

Meditation   Inspiration

Yoga Practice   ....

6.00

7.00

8.00

9.00

10.00

11.00

12.00

13.00

14.00

15.00

16.00

17.00

18.00

19.00

dream space

date:

gratitude is Wisdom...

Meditation
Inspiration

Yoga Practice
....

6.00

Today, I feel **inspired** to do...

7.00

I create my day with my **thoughts**, therefore...

8.00

I AM

I AM

9.00

I AM

10.00

What did I **love** about my yoga practice today?

11.00

12.00

In what ways would I like to **grow**?

13.00

14.00

15.00

What would I like to **let go** of?

16.00

17.00

What was my underlying **motivation** today?

18.00

19.00

weekly check - in

	09.00	13.00	17.00
	10.00	14.00	18.00
	11.00	15.00	19.00
	12.00	16.00	20.00

What projects have I completed this week?

□ Review Conscious Life Blueprint

□ Review Purpose Statement

□ Update 90-Day Planner

What's going well with my practice and why is it?

□ Add Actions to Weekly Planner

□ Plan Your Week

What do I find most challenging in my life right now?

Old Habit >

What is one thing I can do this week that will create the biggest results in my life?

New Habit >

What am I happy about right now?

How can I be more empowered in my thoughts, words and actions?

New Actions >

What fears are holding me back and how can I overcome those?

New Affirmation/Mantra/Yoga Pose

How does my body feel? Am I feeling grounded?

weekly planner

4 Major Goals I'm Focused On This Week:

1	2	3	4

Projects & Appointments For This Week	Target date	Actions & Yoga Practice For This Week	Target date
monday			
tuesday			
wednesday			
thursday			
friday			
saturday			
sunday			

date:

soul space

My Yoga Practice

When I am **grateful** I open up to more...

☐ Meditation   ☐ Inspiration

☐ Yoga Practice   ☐ ....

What would I do **today**, if it was my last?

| 6.00 |
| 7.00 |

Today...
I AM
I AM
I AM

| 8.00 |
| 9.00 |

What was **interesting** about today?

| 10.00 |
| 11.00 |
| 12.00 |

What am I not **seeing**?

| 13.00 |
| 14.00 |

What ideas would I like to **upgrade**?

| 15.00 |
| 16.00 |
| 17.00 |

When was I completely in the **moment** today?

| 18.00 |

| 19.00 |

heart space

date:

Meditation   Inspiration

Yoga Practice   ....

6.00

7.00

8.00

9.00

10.00

11.00

12.00

13.00

14.00

15.00

16.00

17.00

18.00

19.00

Today, I give **thanks** for...

My **inspired** actions for today are...

Today I **honour** how I feel and...

I AM

I AM

I AM

What was today's **lesson**?

How can I create a more **challenging** yoga practice?

What do I **know** that I'm not admitting?

What **strengths** did I use today?

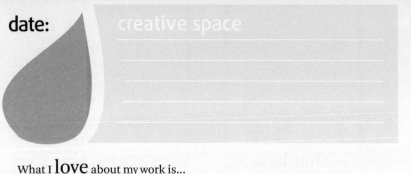

date:

creative space

What I **love** about my work is...

Today I am inspired to take these **actions**:

I have a **beautiful** mind and...

I AM
I AM
I AM

What did I **learn** on the yoga mat today?

How was my **mindset** today?

What new **habit** do I want to adopt into my life?

Where am I at this very moment?

Meditation   Inspiration

Yoga Practice   ....

6.00

7.00

8.00

9.00

10.00

I AM connected to my divine essence

11.00

12.00

13.00

14.00

15.00

16.00

17.00

18.00

19.00

My Yoga Practice

date:

Meditation   Inspiration

Yoga Practice   . . . .

6.00

7.00

8.00

9.00

10.00

11.00

12.00

13.00

14.00

15.00

16.00

17.00

18.00

19.00

I am so grateful for **simple** things like...

What is the best course of **action** to take today?

Today I **am** creative and...

I AM
I AM
I AM

Who AM I?

What am I supposed to do right **now**?

What new **mindset** do I want to adopt into my life?

How did my **yoga** practice feel today?

date:

soul space

My Yoga Practice

Today I am so **grateful** for...

My top 3 **inspired actions** for today are...

My **intentions** for today are...

I AM

I AM

I AM

What did I notice about my **yoga** practice today?

What did I **learn** today?

After today, what **behaviour** do I want to upgrade?

What **strengths** did I use today?

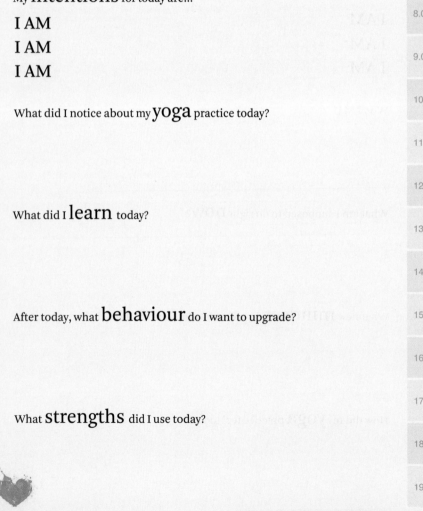

	Meditation		Inspiration
	Yoga Practice		....

6.00

7.00

8.00

9.00

10.00

11.00

12.00

13.00

14.00

15.00

16.00

17.00

18.00

19.00

heart space

date:

My Appreciation & gratitude list

Meditation   Inspiration

Yoga Practice   ....

6.00

7.00

Today, I am most inspired to do...

8.00

The mindset I wish to create today is...

I AM

I AM

9.00

I AM

10.00

What did I enjoy about today?

11.00

12.00

What challenged me today that I can learn from?

13.00

14.00

15.00

What new yoga pose would I like to perfect?

16.00

17.00

What did I do really well today?

18.00

19.00

weekly check - in

	09.00	13.00	17.00
	10.00	14.00	18.00
	11.00	15.00	19.00
	12.00	16.00	20.00

What have I achieved on my Conscious Life Blueprint this week?

■ Review Conscious Life Blueprint

■ Review Purpose Statement

What do I need to start or stop?

■ Update 90-Day Planner

■ Add Actions to Weekly Planner

■ Plan Your Week

In my relationships, how can I communicate better?

Old Habit >

What is one thing I can do this week that will create the biggest results in my life?

New Habit >

What am I proud about right now?

How can I be happier and more grateful?

New Actions >

What negative attitudes are holding me back and how can I overcome those?

New Affirmation/Mantra/Yoga Pos

How can I stretch myself further in my yoga practice?

weekly planner

1	2	3	4

Projects & Appointments For This Week	Target date	Actions & Yoga Practice For This Week	Target date
monday			
tuesday			
wednesday			
thursday			
friday			
saturday			
sunday			

date:

creative space

The things I am **grateful** for in my life are...

Meditation   Inspiration

Yoga Practice   ....

Today, I would **love** to do:

6.00

7.00

Today **i am focusing** on being...

I AM

I AM   8.00

I AM

9.00

What did I notice about my **thoughts** today?

10.00

11.00

12.00

What could I have handled **differently** today?

13.00

14.00

How can I open to **new** possibilities?   15.00

16.00

17.00

What am I **proud** of that came about today?

18.00

19.00

dream space

date:

Meditation   Inspiration

Yoga Practice   ....

6.00

7.00

8.00

9.00

10.00

11.00

12.00

13.00

14.00

15.00

16.00

17.00

18.00

19.00

gratitude is Wisdom...

Today, I feel **inspired** to do...

I AM
pure
awareness

I create my day with my **thoughts**, therefore...

I AM

I AM

I AM

What did I **love** about my yoga practice today?

In what ways would I like to **grow**?

What would I like to **let go** of?

What was my underlying **motivation** today?

date:

soul space

My Yoga Practice

When I am **grateful** I open up to more...

Meditation   Inspiration

Yoga Practice   ....

What would I do **today**, if it was my last?

| 6.00 |

| 7.00 |

Today...

I AM

I AM

I AM

| 8.00 |

| 9.00 |

What was **interesting** about today?

| 10.00 |

| 11.00 |

| 12.00 |

What am I not **seeing**?

| 13.00 |

| 14.00 |

What ideas would I like to **upgrade**?

| 15.00 |

| 16.00 |

| 17.00 |

When was I completely in the **moment** today?

| 18.00 |

| 19.00 |

date:

Meditation   Inspiration

Yoga Practice   ....

6.00

7.00

8.00

9.00

10.00

11.00

12.00

13.00

14.00

15.00

16.00

17.00

18.00

19.00

Today, I give **thanks** for...

My **inspired** actions for today are...

Today I **honour** how I feel and...

I AM

I AM

I AM

What was today's **lesson**?

How can I create a more **challenging** yoga practice?

What do I **know** that I'm not admitting?

What **strengths** did I use today?

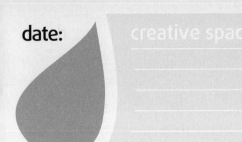

date:

What I **love** about my work is...

Today I am inspired to take these **actions**:

I have a **beautiful** mind and...

I AM

I AM

I AM

What did I **learn** on the yoga mat today?

How was my **mindset** today?

What new **habit** do I want to adopt into my life?

Where am I at this very moment?

My Yoga Practice

■	Meditation	■	Inspiration
■	Yoga Practice	■	....

| 6.00 |
| 7.00 |
| 8.00 |
| 9.00 |
| 10.00 |
| 11.00 |
| 12.00 |
| 13.00 |
| 14.00 |
| 15.00 |
| 16.00 |
| 17.00 |
| 18.00 |
| 19.00 |

My Yoga Practice

dream space   date:

I am so grateful for simple things like...

Meditation   Inspiration

Yoga Practice   ....

What is the best course of action to take today?

6.00

7.00

Today I am creative and...

8.00

I AM

I AM

9.00

I AM

10.00

Who AM I?

11.00

12.00

What am I supposed to do right now?

13.00

14.00

15.00

What new mindset do I want to adopt into my life?

16.00

17.00

How did my yoga practice feel today?

18.00

19.00

weekly check - in

	09.00	13.00	17.00
	10.00	14.00	18.00
	11.00	15.00	19.00
	12.00	16.00	20.00

What major goals have I achieved this month?

How can I be more congruent with my thoughts, words and actions?

What are the biggest distractions to my yoga practice and how can I remove them?

What is one thing I can do this week that will create the biggest results in my life?

What am I committed to in my life right now?

How can I shine my light more?

What disempowering thoughts are holding me back and how can I upgrade those?

What new pose or asana can I incorporate into my current yoga practice?

- Review Conscious Life Blueprint
- Review Purpose Statement
- Update 90-Day Planner
- Add Actions to Weekly Planner
- Plan Your Week

Old Habit >

New Habit >

New Actions >

New Affirmation/Mantra/Yoga Pos

weekly planner

4 Major Goals I'm Focused On This Week:

1	2	3	4

Projects & Appointments For This Week	Target date	Actions & Yoga Practice For This Week	Target date
monday			
tuesday			
wednesday			
thursday			
friday			
saturday			
sunday			

date:

soul space

_____
_____
_____
_____

My Yoga Practice

_____
_____
_____
_____
_____
_____

Today I am so **grateful** for...

I AM
present

My top 3 **inspired actions** for today are...

| Meditation | Inspiration |
| Yoga Practice | .... |

My **intentions** for today are...

I AM

I AM

I AM

What did I notice about my **yoga** practice today?

What did I **learn** today?

After today, what **behaviour** do I want to upgrade?

What **strengths** did I use today?

6.00

7.00

8.00

9.00

10.00

11.00

12.00

13.00

14.00

15.00

16.00

17.00

18.00

19.00

My Yoga Practice

Meditation   Inspiration

Yoga Practice   ....

6.00

7.00

8.00

9.00

10.00

11.00

12.00

13.00

14.00

15.00

16.00

17.00

18.00

19.00

date:

My Appreciation & gratitude list

Today, I am most inspired to do...

The mindset I wish to create today is...

I AM

I AM

I AM

What did I enjoy about today?

What challenged me today that I can learn from?

What new yoga pose would I like to perfect?

What did I do really well today?

date:

The things I am **grateful** for in my life are...

Today, I would **love** to do:

Today **i am focusing** on being...

I AM

I AM

I AM

What did I notice about my **thoughts** today?

What could I have handled **differently** today?

How can I open to **new** possibilities?

What am I **proud** of that came about today?

Meditation   Inspiration

Yoga Practice   ....

6.00

7.00

8.00

9.00

10.00

11.00

12.00

13.00

14.00

15.00

16.00

17.00

18.00

19.00

gratitude is Wisdom...

Meditation   Inspiration

Yoga Practice   ....

6.00

7.00

8.00

9.00

10.00

11.00

12.00

13.00

14.00

15.00

16.00

17.00

18.00

19.00

Today, I feel inspired to do...

I create my day with my thoughts, therefore...

I AM

I AM

I AM

What did I love about my yoga practice today?

In what ways would I like to grow?

What would I like to let go of?

What was my underlying motivation today?

date:

soul space

My Yoga Practice

When I am **grateful** I open up to more...

	Meditation		Inspiration
	Yoga Practice		....

What would I do **today**, if it was my last?

6.00
7.00
8.00

Today...
I AM
I AM
I AM

9.00
10.00

What was **interesting** about today?

11.00
12.00

What am I not **seeing**?

13.00
14.00

What ideas would I like to **upgrade**?

15.00
16.00
17.00

When was I completely in the **moment** today?

18.00
19.00

My Yoga Practice

date:

Today, I give **thanks** for...

Meditation | Inspiration

Yoga Practice | ....

My **inspired** actions for today are...

6.00

7.00

Today I **honour** how I feel and...

8.00

I AM

I AM

9.00

I AM

10.00

What was today's **lesson**?

11.00

12.00

How can I create a more **challenging** yoga practice?

13.00

14.00

15.00

What do I **know** that I'm not admitting?

16.00

17.00

What **strengths** did I use today?

18.00

19.00

weekly check - in

	09.00	13.00	17.00
	10.00	14.00	18.00
	11.00	15.00	19.00
	12.00	16.00	20.00

What have I achieved this week?

What's working with my practice and why is it working?

What's not working and what am I willing to do to upgrade it?

What is one thing I can do this week that will create the biggest results in my life?

What do I need to make a decision about?

How can I be more authentic?

What beliefs are holding me back and how can I upgrade them?

How can I open my chakras for more connection to my source?

- Review Conscious Life Blueprint
- Review Purpose Statement
- Update 90-Day Planner
- Add Actions to Weekly Planner
- Plan Your Week

Old Habit >

New Habit >

New Actions >

New Affirmation/Mantra/Yoga Pose

weekly planner

4 Major Goals I'm Focused On This Week:

1	2	3	4

Projects & Appointments For This Week	Target date	Actions & Yoga Practice For This Week	Target date
monday			
tuesday			
wednesday			
thursday			
friday			
saturday			
sunday			

date:

creative space

What I love about my work is...

Today I am inspired to take these **actions**:

I have a **beautiful** mind and...

I AM

I AM

I AM

What did I **learn** on the yoga mat today?

How was my **mindset** today?

What new **habit** do I want to adopt into my life?

Where am I at this very moment?

My Yoga Practice

| | Meditation | | Inspiration |
| | Yoga Practice | | .... |

6.00

7.00

8.00

9.00

10.00

11.00

12.00

13.00

14.00

15.00

16.00

17.00

18.00

19.00

My Yoga Practice

dream space

date:

I am so grateful for **simple** things like...

■ Meditation	■ Inspiration
■ Yoga Practice	■ ....

What is the best course of **action** to take today?

6.00

7.00

Today I **am** creative and...

I AM

I AM

I AM

8.00

9.00

10.00

Who AM I?

I AM
empowered

11.00

12.00

What am I supposed to do right **now**?

13.00

14.00

What new **mindset** do I want to adopt into my life?

15.00

16.00

17.00

How did my **yoga** practice feel today?

18.00

19.00

date:

soul space

My Yoga Practice

Today I am so **grateful** for...

My top 3 **inspired actions** for today are...

My **intentions** for today are...

I AM

I AM

I AM

What did I notice about my **yoga** practice today?

What did I **learn** today?

After today, what **behaviour** do I want to upgrade?

What **strengths** did I use today?

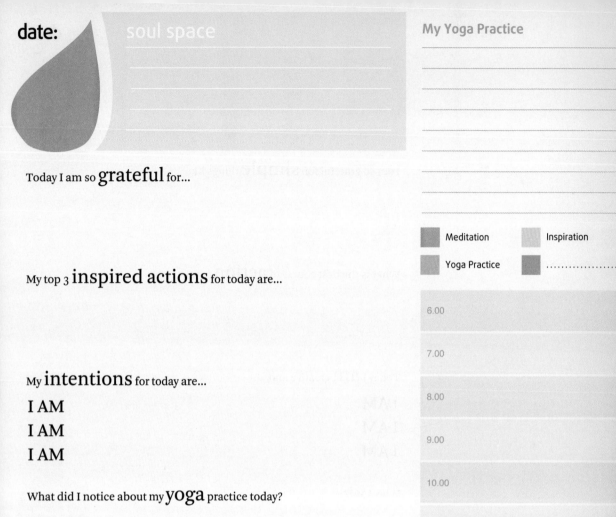

Meditation   Inspiration

Yoga Practice   ....

6.00

7.00

8.00

9.00

10.00

11.00

12.00

13.00

14.00

15.00

16.00

17.00

18.00

19.00

My Yoga Practice

date:

My Appreciation & gratitude list

☐ Meditation   ☐ Inspiration

☐ Yoga Practice   ☐ ....

Today, I am most inspired to do...

6.00

7.00

The mindset I wish to create today is...

I AM

I AM

8.00

I AM

9.00

What did I enjoy about today?

10.00

11.00

12.00

What challenged me today that I can learn from?

13.00

14.00

15.00   What new yoga pose would I like to perfect?

16.00

17.00   What did I do really well today?

18.00

19.00

date:

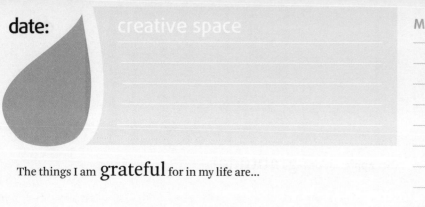

The things I am **grateful** for in my life are...

Today, I would **love** to do:

Today **i am focusing** on being...

I AM

I AM

I AM

What did I notice about my **thoughts** today?

What could I have handled **differently** today?

How can I open to **new** possibilities?

What am I **proud** of that came about today?

My Yoga Practice

Meditation   Inspiration

Yoga Practice   ....

6.00

7.00

8.00

9.00

10.00

11.00

12.00

13.00

14.00

15.00

16.00

17.00

18.00

19.00

date:

gratitude is Wisdom...

Meditation	Inspiration
Yoga Practice	....

6.00

Today, I feel inspired to do...

7.00

8.00

I create my day with my thoughts, therefore...

I AM

I AM

9.00

I AM

10.00

What did I love about my yoga practice today?

11.00

12.00

In what ways would I like to grow?

13.00

14.00

15.00

What would I like to let go of?

16.00

17.00

What was my underlying motivation today?

18.00

19.00

weekly check - in

	09.00	13.00	17.00
	10.00	14.00	18.00
	11.00	15.00	19.00
	12.00	16.00	20.00

What projects have I completed this week?

What's going well with my practice and why is it?

What do I find most challenging in my life right now?

What is one thing I can do this week that will create the biggest results in my life?

What am I happy about right now?

How can I be more empowered in my thoughts, words and actions?

What fears are holding me back and how can I overcome those?

How does my body feel? Am I feeling grounded?

Review Conscious Life Blueprint

Review Purpose Statement

Update 90-Day Planner

Add Actions to Weekly Planner

Plan Your Week

Old Habit >

New Habit >

New Actions >

New Affirmation/Mantra/Yoga Pos

weekly planner

| 1 | 2 | 3 | 4 |

Projects & Appointments For This Week	Target date	Actions & Yoga Practice For This Week	Target date
monday			
tuesday			
wednesday			
thursday			
friday			
saturday			
sunday			

date:

When I am **grateful** I open up to more...

What would I do **today**, if it was my last?

Today...
I AM
I AM
I AM

What was **interesting** about today?

What am I not **seeing**?

What ideas would I like to **upgrade**?

When was I completely in the **moment** today?

My Yoga Practice

Meditation   Inspiration

Yoga Practice   ....

6.00

7.00

8.00

9.00

10.00

11.00

12.00

I AM
awake

13.00

14.00

15.00

16.00

17.00

18.00

19.00

date:

Meditation

Inspiration

Yoga Practice

. . . .

6.00

7.00

8.00

9.00

10.00

11.00

12.00

13.00

14.00

15.00

16.00

17.00

18.00

19.00

Today, I give **thanks** for...

My **inspired** actions for today are...

Today I **honour** how I feel and...

I AM

I AM

I AM

What was today's **lesson**?

How can I create a more **challenging** yoga practice?

What do I **know** that I'm not admitting?

What **strengths** did I use today?

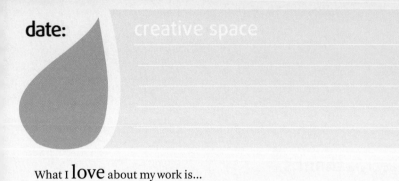

date:

creative space

What I love about my work is...

Today I am inspired to take these actions:

I have a beautiful mind and...

I AM

I AM

I AM

What did I learn on the yoga mat today?

How was my mindset today?

What new habit do I want to adopt into my life?

Where am I at this very moment?

Meditation   Inspiration

Yoga Practice   ....

6.00	
7.00	
8.00	
9.00	
10.00	
11.00	
12.00	
13.00	
14.00	
15.00	
16.00	
17.00	
18.00	
19.00	

dream space

date:

I am so grateful for **simple** things like...

Meditation

Inspiration

Yoga Practice

....

6.00

7.00

What is the best course of **action** to take today?

8.00

Today I **am** creative and...

I AM

I AM

9.00

I AM

10.00

Who AM I?

11.00

12.00

What am I supposed to do right **now**?

13.00

14.00

15.00

What new **mindset** do I want to adopt into my life?

16.00

17.00

How did my **yoga** practice feel today?

18.00

19.00

date:

Today I am so **grateful** for...

My top 3 **inspired actions** for today are...

My **intentions** for today are...

I AM

I AM

I AM

What did I notice about my **yoga** practice today?

What did I **learn** today?

After today, what **behaviour** do I want to upgrade?

What **strengths** did I use today?

My Yoga Practice

■ Meditation	■ Inspiration
■ Yoga Practice	■ ....

6.00	
7.00	
8.00	
9.00	
10.00	
11.00	
12.00	
13.00	
14.00	
15.00	
16.00	
17.00	
18.00	
19.00	

heart space

date:

My Appreciation & gratitude list

Meditation   Inspiration

Yoga Practice   ....

6.00

7.00

Today, I am most inspired to do...

8.00

9.00

The mindset I wish to create today is...

I AM

I AM

I AM

10.00

11.00

What did I enjoy about today?

12.00

13.00

What challenged me today that I can learn from?

14.00

15.00

What new yoga pose would I like to perfect?

16.00

17.00

What did I do really well today?

18.00

19.00

weekly check - in

	09.00	13.00	17.00
	10.00	14.00	18.00
	11.00	15.00	19.00
	12.00	16.00	20.00

What have I achieved on my Conscious Life Blueprint this week?

What do I need to start or stop?

In my relationships, how can I communicate better?

What is one thing I can do this week that will create the biggest results in my life?

What am I proud about right now?

How can I be happier and more grateful?

What negative attitudes are holding me back and how can I overcome those?

How can I stretch myself further in my yoga practice?

- Review Conscious Life Blueprint
- Review Purpose Statement
- Update 90-Day Planner
- Add Actions to Weekly Planner
- Plan Your Week

Old Habit >

New Habit >

New Actions >

New Affirmation/Mantra/Yoga Pos

weekly planner

4 Major Goals I'm Focused On This Week:

1	2	3	4

Projects & Appointments For This Week	Target date	Actions & Yoga Practice For This Week	Target date
monday			
tuesday			
wednesday			
thursday			
friday			
saturday			
sunday			

date:

creative space

The things I am grateful for in my life are...

Meditation   Inspiration

Yoga Practice   ....

Today, I would love to do:

Today i am focusing on being...

I AM

I AM

I AM

What did I notice about my thoughts today?

What could I have handled differently today?

How can I open to new possibilities?

What am I proud of that came about today?

6.00

7.00

8.00

9.00

10.00

11.00

12.00

13.00

14.00

15.00

16.00

17.00

18.00

19.00

dream space

date:

_____

_____

_____

_____

gratitude is Wisdom...

Meditation   Inspiration

Yoga Practice   ....

Today, I feel inspired to do...

| | 6.00 |

| | 7.00 |

I create my day with my thoughts, therefore...

I AM

I AM

I AM

| | 8.00 |

| | 9.00 |

| | 10.00 |

What did I love about my yoga practice today?

| | 11.00 |

| | 12.00 |

In what ways would I like to grow?

| | 13.00 |

I AM conscious

| | 14.00 |

| | 15.00 |

What would I like to let go of?

| | 16.00 |

| | 17.00 |

What was my underlying motivation today?

| | 18.00 |

| | 19.00 |

date:

soul space

When I am grateful I open up to more...

What would I do today, if it was my last?

Today...

I AM

I AM

I AM

What was interesting about today?

What am I not seeing?

What ideas would I like to upgrade?

When was I completely in the moment today?

Meditation   Inspiration

Yoga Practice   ....

6.00

7.00

8.00

9.00

10.00

11.00

12.00

13.00

14.00

15.00

16.00

17.00

18.00

19.00

heart space

date:

Today, I give **thanks** for...

Meditation   Inspiration

Yoga Practice   ....

My **inspired** actions for today are...

Today I **honour** how I feel and...

I AM

I AM

I AM

What was today's **lesson**?

How can I create a more **challenging** yoga practice?

What do I **know** that I'm not admitting?

What **strengths** did I use today?

6.00
7.00
8.00
9.00
10.00
11.00
12.00
13.00
14.00
15.00
16.00
17.00
18.00
19.00

date:

My Yoga Practice

What I **love** about my work is...

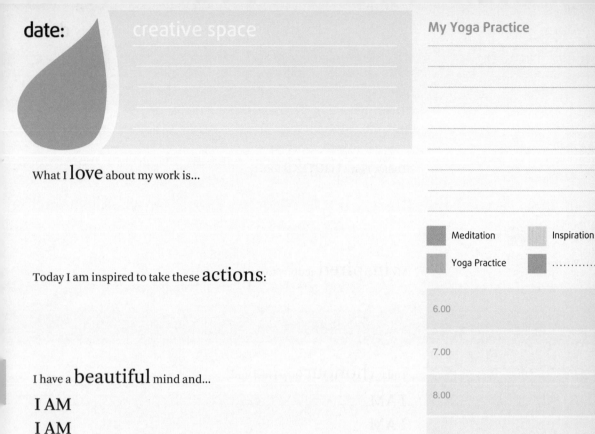

Meditation   Inspiration

Yoga Practice   ....

Today I am inspired to take these **actions**:

6.00

7.00

I have a **beautiful** mind and...
8.00

I AM

I AM
9.00

I AM

What did I **learn** on the yoga mat today?
10.00

11.00

12.00

How was my **mindset** today?
13.00

14.00

What new **habit** do I want to adopt into my life?
15.00

16.00

17.00

Where am I at this very moment?

18.00

19.00

I am so grateful for **simple** things like...

Meditation   Inspiration

Yoga Practice   ....

What is the best course of **action** to take today?

6.00

7.00

Today I **am** creative and...

8.00

I AM
I AM
I AM

9.00

10.00

Who AM I?

11.00

12.00

What am I supposed to do right **now**?

13.00

14.00

15.00

What new **mindset** do I want to adopt into my life?

16.00

17.00

How did my **yoga** practice feel today?

18.00

19.00

weekly check - in

	09.00	13.00	17.00
	10.00	14.00	18.00
	11.00	15.00	19.00
	12.00	16.00	20.00

What major goals have I achieved this month?

How can I be more congruent with my thoughts, words and actions?

What are the biggest distractions to my yoga practice and how can I remove them?

What is one thing I can do this week that will create the biggest results in my life?

What am I committed to in my life right now?

How can I shine my light more?

What disempowering thoughts are holding me back and how can I upgrade those?

What new pose or asana can I incorporate into my current yoga practice?

- Review Conscious Life Blueprint
- Review Purpose Statement
- Update 90-Day Planner
- Add Actions to Weekly Planner
- Plan Your Week

Old Habit >

New Habit >

New Actions >

New Affirmation/Mantra/Yoga Pos

weekly planner

| 1 | 2 | 3 | 4 |

Projects & Appointments For This Week	Target date	Actions & Yoga Practice For This Week	Target date
monday			
tuesday			
wednesday			
thursday			
friday			
saturday			
sunday			

date:

soul space

Today I am so **grateful** for...

My top 3 **inspired actions** for today are...

My **intentions** for today are...

I AM

I AM

I AM

What did I notice about my **yoga** practice today?

What did I **learn** today?

After today, what **behaviour** do I want to upgrade?

What **strengths** did I use today?

My Yoga Practice

Meditation   Inspiration

Yoga Practice   ....

6.00

7.00

8.00

9.00

10.00

11.00

12.00

13.00

14.00

15.00

16.00

17.00

18.00

19.00

date:

My Appreciation & gratitude list

Meditation   Inspiration

Yoga Practice   ....

Today, I am most inspired to do...

6.00

7.00

The mindset I wish to create today is...

I AM

I AM

8.00

I AM

9.00

10.00

What did I enjoy about today?

11.00

12.00

What challenged me today that I can learn from?

13.00

14.00

15.00

What new yoga pose would I like to perfect?

16.00

17.00

What did I do really well today?

18.00

19.00

date:

creative space

The things I am **grateful** for in my life are...

Today, I would **love** to do:

Today **i am focusing** on being...

I AM

I AM

I AM

What did I notice about my **thoughts** today?

What could I have handled **differently** today?

How can I open to **new** possibilities?

What am I **proud** of that came about today?

Meditation   Inspiration

Yoga Practice   ....

6.00

7.00

8.00

9.00

10.00

11.00

12.00

13.00

14.00

15.00

16.00

17.00

18.00

19.00

dream space

date:

gratitude is Wisdom...

Meditation   Inspiration

Yoga Practice   ....

6.00

7.00

Today, I feel **inspired** to do...

8.00

I create my day with my **thoughts**, therefore...

I AM

I AM

9.00

I AM

10.00

What did I **love** about my yoga practice today?

11.00

12.00

In what ways would I like to **grow**?

13.00

14.00

15.00

What would I like to **let go** of?

16.00

17.00

What was my underlying **motivation** today?

18.00

19.00

date:

soul space

When I am **grateful** I open up to more...

What would I do **today**, if it was my last?

Today...
I AM
I AM
I AM

What was **interesting** about today?

What am I not **seeing**?

What ideas would I like to **upgrade**?

When was I completely in the **moment** today?

My Yoga Practice

Meditation	Inspiration
Yoga Practice	....

6.00

7.00

8.00

9.00

10.00

11.00

12.00

13.00

14.00

15.00

16.00

17.00

18.00

19.00

Meditation   Inspiration

Yoga Practice   . . . .

Today, I give **thanks** for...

My **inspired** actions for today are...

6.00	
7.00	

Today I **honour** how I feel and...

I AM

I AM

I AM

What was today's **lesson**?

How can I create a more **challenging** yoga practice?

What do I **know** that I'm not admitting?

What **strengths** did I use today?

6.00

7.00

8.00

9.00

10.00

11.00

12.00

13.00

14.00

15.00

16.00

17.00

18.00

19.00

weekly check - in

	09.00	13.00	17.00
	10.00	14.00	18.00
	11.00	15.00	19.00
	12.00	16.00	20.00

What have I achieved this week?

What's working with my practice and why is it working?

What's not working and what am I willing to do to upgrade it?

What is one thing I can do this week that will create the biggest results in my life?

What do I need to make a decision about?

How can I be more authentic?

What beliefs are holding me back and how can I upgrade them?

How can I open my chakras for more connection to my source?

Review Conscious Life Blueprint

Review Purpose Statement

Update 90-Day Planner

Add Actions to Weekly Planner

Plan Your Week

Old Habit >

New Habit >

New Actions >

New Affirmation/Mantra/Yoga Pos

weekly planner

1	2	3	4

Projects & Appointments For This Week	Target date	Actions & Yoga Practice For This Week	Target date
monday			
tuesday			
wednesday			
thursday			
friday			
saturday			
sunday			

date:

What I **love** about my work is...

Today I am inspired to take these **actions**:

I have a **beautiful** mind and...

I AM

I AM

I AM

What did I **learn** on the yoga mat today?

How was my **mindset** today?

What new **habit** do I want to adopt into my life?

Where am I at this very moment?

My Yoga Practice

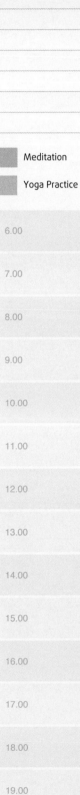

Meditation   Inspiration

Yoga Practice   ....

6.00

7.00

8.00

9.00

10.00

11.00

12.00

13.00

14.00

15.00

16.00

17.00

18.00

19.00

My Yoga Practice

dream space

date:

I am so grateful for **simple** things like...

Meditation   Inspiration

Yoga Practice   ....

What is the best course of **action** to take today?

6.00

7.00

Today I **am** creative and...

I AM

I AM

8.00

I AM

9.00

Who AM I?

10.00

11.00

12.00

What am I supposed to do right **now**?

13.00

14.00

What new **mindset** do I want to adopt into my life?

15.00

16.00

17.00

How did my **yoga** practice feel today?

18.00

19.00

date:

soul space

Today I am so **grateful** for...

Meditation   Inspiration

Yoga Practice   ....

My top 3 **inspired actions** for today are...

6.00

7.00

My **intentions** for today are...

I AM

I AM

I AM

8.00

9.00

What did I notice about my **yoga** practice today?

10.00

11.00

12.00

What did I **learn** today?

13.00

I AM
happy,
healthy &
connected

14.00

After today, what **behaviour** do I want to upgrade?

15.00

16.00

17.00

What **strengths** did I use today?

18.00

19.00

My Yoga Practice

_____
_____
_____
_____
_____
_____
_____
_____

| | Meditation | | Inspiration |
| | Yoga Practice | | .... |

6.00

7.00

8.00

9.00

10.00

11.00

12.00

13.00

14.00

15.00

16.00

17.00

18.00

19.00

heart space

date:

My Appreciation & gratitude list

Today, I am most inspired to do...

The mindset I wish to create today is...

I AM

I AM

I AM

What did I enjoy about today?

What challenged me today that I can learn from?

What new yoga pose would I like to perfect?

What did I do really well today?

date:

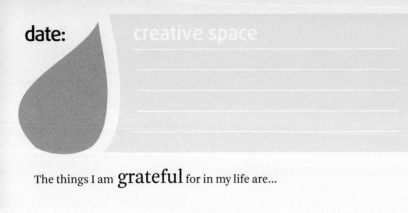

creative space

The things I am **grateful** for in my life are...

Today, I would **love** to do:

Today **i am focusing** on being...

I AM

I AM

I AM

What did I notice about my **thoughts** today?

What could I have handled **differently** today?

How can I open to **new** possibilities?

What am I **proud** of that came about today?

Meditation Inspiration

Yoga Practice ....

6.00

7.00

8.00

9.00

10.00

11.00

12.00

13.00

14.00

15.00

16.00

17.00

18.00

19.00

date:

gratitude is Wisdom...

	Meditation		Inspiration
	Yoga Practice		....

6.00

7.00

8.00

9.00

10.00

11.00

12.00

13.00

14.00

15.00

16.00

17.00

18.00

19.00

Today, I feel inspired to do...

I create my day with my thoughts, therefore...

I AM

I AM

I AM

What did I love about my yoga practice today?

In what ways would I like to grow?

What would I like to let go of?

What was my underlying motivation today?

weekly check - in

	09.00	13.00	17.00
	10.00	14.00	18.00
	11.00	15.00	19.00
	12.00	16.00	20.00

What projects have I completed this week?

What's going well with my practice and why is it?

What do I find most challenging in my life right now?

What is one thing I can do this week that will create the biggest results in my life?

What am I happy about right now?

How can I be more empowered in my thoughts, words and actions?

What fears are holding me back and how can I overcome those?

How does my body feel? Am I feeling grounded?

Review Conscious Life Blueprint

Review Purpose Statement

Update 90-Day Planner

Add Actions to Weekly Planner

Plan Your Week

Old Habit >

New Habit >

New Actions >

New Affirmation/Mantra/Yoga Pose

weekly planner

1	2	3	4

Projects & Appointments For This Week	Target date	Actions & Yoga Practice For This Week	Target date
monday			
tuesday			
wednesday			
thursday			
friday			
saturday			
sunday			

date:

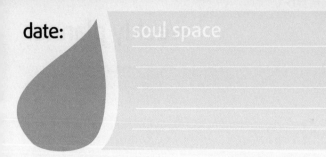

soul space

When I am **grateful** I open up to more...

Meditation	Inspiration
Yoga Practice	....

What would I do **today**, if it was my last?

6.00

7.00

Today...

I AM

8.00

I AM

I AM

9.00

What was **interesting** about today?

10.00

11.00

12.00

What am I not **seeing**?

13.00

14.00

What ideas would I like to **upgrade**?

15.00

16.00

17.00

When was I completely in the **moment** today?

18.00

19.00

My Yoga Practice

heart space

date:

Today, I give **thanks** for...

Meditation   Inspiration

Yoga Practice   ....

My **inspired** actions for today are...

6.00

7.00

Today I **honour** how I feel and...

I AM

I AM

8.00

I AM

9.00

What was today's **lesson**?

10.00

11.00

12.00

How can I create a more **challenging** yoga practice?

13.00

14.00

15.00

What do I **know** that I'm not admitting?

16.00

17.00

What **strengths** did I use today?

18.00

19.00

date:

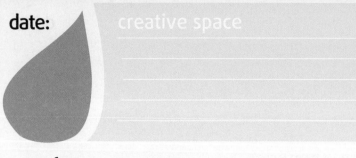

creative space

What I **love** about my work is...

Today I am inspired to take these **actions**:

I have a **beautiful** mind and...

I AM

I AM

I AM

What did I **learn** on the yoga mat today?

How was my **mindset** today?

What new **habit** do I want to adopt into my life?

Where am I at this very moment?

My Yoga Practice

Meditation		Inspiration
Yoga Practice		....

6.00	
7.00	
8.00	
9.00	
10.00	
11.00	
12.00	
13.00	
14.00	
15.00	
16.00	
17.00	
18.00	
19.00	

I am so grateful for **simple** things like...

What is the best course of **action** to take today?

6.00

7.00

Today I **am** creative and...

I AM

I AM

8.00

I AM

9.00

Who AM I?

10.00

11.00

12.00

What am I supposed to do right **now**?

13.00

14.00

15.00

What new **mindset** do I want to adopt into my life?

16.00

17.00

How did my **yoga** practice feel today?

18.00

19.00

date:

soul space

My Yoga Practice

Today I am so **grateful** for...

■ Meditation   ▦ Inspiration

■ Yoga Practice   ■ ....

My top 3 **inspired actions** for today are...

6.00

7.00

My **intentions** for today are...

I AM

I AM

8.00

I AM

9.00

What did I notice about my **yoga** practice today?

10.00

11.00

12.00

What did I **learn** today?

13.00

14.00

After today, what **behaviour** do I want to upgrade?

15.00

16.00

17.00

What **strengths** did I use today?

18.00

19.00

heart space

date:

My Appreciation & gratitude list

Meditation   Inspiration

Yoga Practice   ....

Today, I am most inspired to do...

6.00

7.00

The mindset I wish to create today is...

I AM

8.00

I AM

9.00

I AM

10.00

What did I enjoy about today?

11.00

12.00

What challenged me today that I can learn from?

13.00

14.00

What new yoga pose would I like to perfect?

15.00

16.00

17.00

What did I do really well today?

18.00

19.00

weekly check - in

	09.00	13.00	17.00
	10.00	14.00	18.00
	11.00	15.00	19.00
	12.00	16.00	20.00

What have I achieved on my Conscious Life Blueprint this week?

What do I need to start or stop?

In my relationships, how can I communicate better?

What is one thing I can do this week that will create the biggest results in my life?

What am I proud about right now?

How can I be happier and more grateful?

What negative attitudes are holding me back and how can I overcome those?

How can I stretch myself further in my yoga practice?

■ Review Conscious Life Blueprint

■ Review Purpose Statement

■ Update 90-Day Planner

■ Add Actions to Weekly Planner

■ Plan Your Week

Old Habit >

New Habit >

New Actions >

New Affirmation/Mantra/Yoga Pose

weekly planner

4 Major Goals I'm Focused On This Week:			
1	2	3	4

Projects & Appointments For This Week	Target date	Actions & Yoga Practice For This Week	Target date
monday			
tuesday			
wednesday			
thursday			
friday			
saturday			
sunday			

date:

creative space

The things I am grateful for in my life are...

Today, I would love to do:

Today i am focusing on being...

I AM

I AM

I AM

What did I notice about my thoughts today?

What could I have handled differently today?

How can I open to new possibilities?

What am I proud of that came about today?

Meditation   Inspiration

Yoga Practice   ....

6.00

7.00

8.00

9.00

10.00

11.00

12.00

13.00

14.00

15.00

16.00

17.00

18.00

19.00

dream space

date:

gratitude is Wisdom...

Meditation   Inspiration

Yoga Practice   ....

6.00

7.00

8.00

9.00

10.00

11.00

12.00

13.00

14.00

15.00

16.00

17.00

18.00

19.00

Today, I feel **inspired** to do...

I create my day with my **thoughts**, therefore...

I AM

I AM

I AM

What did I **love** about my yoga practice today?

In what ways would I like to **grow**?

What would I like to **let go** of?

I AM awakening to my potential

What was my underlying **motivation** today?

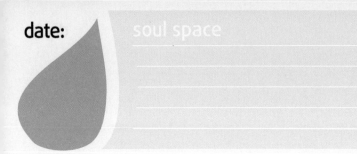

date:

soul space

My Yoga Practice

When I am **grateful** I open up to more...

What would I do **today**, if it was my last?

6.00

7.00

Today...

I AM

I AM

I AM

8.00

9.00

10.00

What was **interesting** about today?

11.00

12.00

What am I not **seeing**?

13.00

14.00

What ideas would I like to **upgrade**?

15.00

16.00

17.00

When was I completely in the **moment** today?

18.00

19.00

heart space

date:

Meditation

Inspiration

Yoga Practice

....

6.00

7.00

8.00

9.00

10.00

11.00

12.00

13.00

14.00

15.00

16.00

17.00

18.00

19.00

Today, I give **thanks** for...

My **inspired** actions for today are...

Today I **honour** how I feel and...

I AM

I AM

I AM

What was today's **lesson**?

How can I create a more **challenging** yoga practice?

What do I **know** that I'm not admitting?

What **strengths** did I use today?

date:

What I **love** about my work is…

Today I am inspired to take these **actions**:

I have a **beautiful** mind and…

I AM

I AM

I AM

What did I **learn** on the yoga mat today?

How was my **mindset** today?

What new **habit** do I want to adopt into my life?

Where am I at this very moment?

My Yoga Practice

Meditation   Inspiration

Yoga Practice   ....

6.00

7.00

8.00

9.00

10.00

11.00

12.00

13.00

14.00

15.00

16.00

17.00

18.00

19.00

date:

I am so grateful for simple things like...

Meditation   Inspiration

Yoga Practice   ....

6.00

What is the best course of action to take today?

7.00

8.00

Today I am creative and...

I AM

9.00

I AM

I AM

10.00

Who AM I?

11.00

12.00

13.00

What am I supposed to do right now?

14.00

15.00

What new mindset do I want to adopt into my life?

16.00

17.00

How did my yoga practice feel today?

18.00

19.00

weekly check - in

	09.00	13.00	17.00
	10.00	14.00	18.00
	11.00	15.00	19.00
	12.00	16.00	20.00

What major goals have I achieved this month?

How can I be more congruent with my thoughts, words and actions?

What are the biggest distractions to my yoga practice and how can I remove them?

What is one thing I can do this week that will create the biggest results in my life?

What am I committed to in my life right now?

How can I shine my light more?

What disempowering thoughts are holding me back and how can I upgrade those?

What new pose or asana can I incorporate into my current yoga practice?

☐ Review Conscious Life Blueprint

☐ Review Purpose Statement

☐ Update 90-Day Planner

☐ Add Actions to Weekly Planner

☐ Plan Your Week

Old Habit >

New Habit >

New Actions >

New Affirmation/Mantra/Yoga Pose

weekly planner

1	2	3	4

Projects & Appointments For This Week	Target date	Actions & Yoga Practice For This Week	Target date
monday			
tuesday			
wednesday			
thursday			
friday			
saturday			
sunday			

date:

soul space

My Yoga Practice

Today I am so grateful for...

My top 3 inspired actions for today are...

| Meditation | | Inspiration |
| Yoga Practice | | .... |

6.00

7.00

My intentions for today are...

I AM

I AM

I AM

8.00

9.00

What did I notice about my yoga practice today?

10.00

11.00

12.00

What did I learn today?

13.00

14.00

After today, what behaviour do I want to upgrade?

15.00

16.00

17.00

What strengths did I use today?

18.00

19.00

date:

My Appreciation & gratitude list

Meditation   Inspiration

Yoga Practice   ....

6.00

7.00

Today, I am most inspired to do...

8.00

9.00

The mindset I wish to create today is...

I AM

I AM

I AM

10.00

What did I enjoy about today?

11.00

12.00

What challenged me today that I can learn from?

13.00

14.00

15.00

What new yoga pose would I like to perfect?

16.00

17.00

What did I do really well today?

18.00

19.00

date:

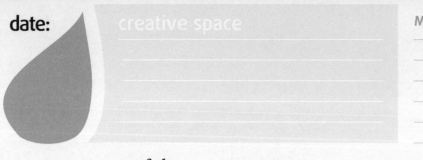

creative space

The things I am grateful for in my life are...

Today, I would love to do:

Today i am focusing on being...

I AM

I AM

I AM

What did I notice about my thoughts today?

What could I have handled differently today?

How can I open to new possibilities?

What am I proud of that came about today?

Meditation   Inspiration

Yoga Practice   ....

6.00

7.00

8.00

9.00

10.00

11.00

12.00

13.00

14.00

15.00

16.00

17.00

18.00

19.00

My Yoga Practice

dream space

date:

☐ Meditation   ☐ Inspiration

☐ Yoga Practice ☐ ....

6.00

7.00

8.00

9.00

10.00

11.00

12.00

13.00

14.00

15.00

16.00

17.00

18.00

19.00

gratitude is Wisdom...

Today, I feel **inspired** to do...

I create my day with my **thoughts**, therefore...

I AM
I AM
I AM

What did I **love** about my yoga practice today?

In what ways would I like to **grow**?

What would I like to **let go** of?

I AM awakening to my potential

What was my underlying **motivation** today?

date:

soul space

When I am **grateful** I open up to more...

Meditation   Inspiration

Yoga Practice   ....

What would I do **today**, if it was my last?

6.00

7.00

Today...

I AM

I AM

I AM

8.00

9.00

10.00

What was **interesting** about today?

11.00

12.00

What am I not **seeing**?

13.00

14.00

What ideas would I like to **upgrade**?

15.00

16.00

17.00

When was I completely in the **moment** today?

18.00

19.00

date:

Meditation   Inspiration

Yoga Practice   . . . .

6.00

7.00

8.00

9.00

10.00

11.00

12.00

13.00

14.00

15.00

16.00

17.00

18.00

19.00

Today, I give **thanks** for...

My **inspired** actions for today are...

Today I **honour** how I feel and...

I AM

I AM

I AM

What was today's **lesson**?

How can I create a more **challenging** yoga practice?

What do I **know** that I'm not admitting?

What **strengths** did I use today?

90 day check-in

Welcome to your 90-day check-in! It's time to celebrate your achievements, identify what needs attention and reset your focus for the next 90 days. Use the answers to the following questions to plan your next quarter and to stay inspired and motivated towards your goals.

What major goals have I achieved this past 90 days?
What am I happy about?

Does my vision still inspire me or do I need to create a new one?
How can I be more aligned with my Conscious Life Blueprint?

What new potentials have I witnessed unfolding
in my life in the last 90 days?

What new mindset do I wish to develop?
What is no longer acceptable to me?

Am I embracing change or resisting it?
How can I open up to more inner expansion?

Am I honouring myself with enough self-love,
self-respect, self-care? How can I love myself more?
What do I need to say yes or no to?

What goal or project am I focusing on for the next 90 days?

What would I love to consciously create over the next 90 days?

Review Conscious Life Blueprint   Review Your Yearly Planner   Plan Your Week

Review Purpose Statement   Complete Next 90 Day Planner   Celebrate Your Progress!

Month:

Goal:

Target date:

Actions to complete this goal:

1.

2.

3.

4.

Why I'd love to achieve this goal:

How will I feel when I've reached this goal?

Goal:

Target date:

Actions to complete this goal:

1.

2.

3.

4.

Why I'd love to achieve this goal:

How will I feel when I've reached this goal?

Goal:

Target date:

Actions to complete this goal:

1.

2.

3.

4.

Why I'd love to achieve this goal:

How will I feel when I've reached this goal?

Goal:

Target date:

Actions to complete this goal:

1.

2.

3.

4.

Why I'd love to achieve this goal:

How will I feel when I've reached this goal?

Month:

Do not feel lonely, the entire universe is inside you.

★ ★ ★

Rumi

Soul Space

weekly planner

1 **2** **3** **4**

Projects & Appointments For This Week	Target date	Actions & Yoga Practice For This Week	Target date
monday			
tuesday			
wednesday			
thursday			
friday			
saturday			
sunday			

date:

soul space

My Yoga Practice

Today I am so **grateful** for...

■	Meditation	■	Inspiration
■	Yoga Practice	■	....

My top 3 **inspired actions** for today are...

My **intentions** for today are...

I AM

I AM

I AM

What did I notice about my **yoga** practice today?

What did I **learn** today?

After today, what **behaviour** do I want to upgrade?

What **strengths** did I use today?

6.00

7.00

8.00

9.00

10.00

11.00

12.00

13.00

14.00

15.00

16.00

17.00

18.00

19.00

date:

My Appreciation & gratitude list

Meditation   Inspiration

Yoga Practice   ....

Today, I am most inspired to do...

6.00

7.00

The mindset I wish to create today is...

8.00

I AM

I AM

9.00

I AM

10.00

What did I enjoy about today?

11.00

12.00

What challenged me today that I can learn from?

13.00

14.00

15.00

What new yoga pose would I like to perfect?

16.00

17.00

What did I do really well today?

18.00

19.00

date:

creative space

My Yoga Practice

The things I am grateful for in my life are...

Today, I would love to do:

Today i am focusing on being...

I AM

I AM

I AM

What did I notice about my thoughts today?

What could I have handled differently today?

How can I open to new possibilities?

What am I proud of that came about today?

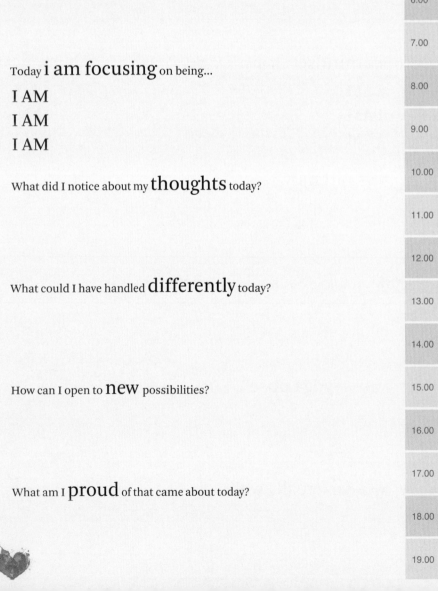

Meditation   Inspiration

Yoga Practice   ....

6.00

7.00

8.00

9.00

10.00

11.00

12.00

13.00

14.00

15.00

16.00

17.00

18.00

19.00

date:

gratitude is Wisdom...

Meditation | Inspiration

Yoga Practice | ....

6.00

7.00

8.00

9.00

10.00

11.00

12.00

13.00

14.00

15.00

16.00

17.00

18.00

19.00

Today, I feel **inspired** to do...

I create my day with my **thoughts**, therefore...

I AM

I AM

I AM

What did I **love** about my yoga practice today?

In what ways would I like to **grow**?

What would I like to **let go** of?

What was my underlying **motivation** today?

I AM happy, healthy & connected

date:

soul space

_____
_____
_____
_____

My Yoga Practice

When I am grateful I open up to more...

What would I do today, if it was my last?

Today...
I AM
I AM
I AM

What was interesting about today?

What am I not seeing?

What ideas would I like to upgrade?

When was I completely in the moment today?

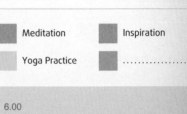

Meditation   Inspiration

Yoga Practice   ....

6.00	
7.00	
8.00	
9.00	
10.00	
11.00	
12.00	
13.00	
14.00	
15.00	
16.00	
17.00	
18.00	
19.00	

date:

Meditation   Inspiration

Yoga Practice   . . . .

6.00

7.00

8.00

9.00

10.00

11.00

12.00

13.00

14.00

15.00

16.00

17.00

18.00

19.00

Today, I give **thanks** for...

My **inspired** actions for today are...

Today I **honour** how I feel and...

I AM

I AM

I AM

What was today's **lesson**?

How can I create a more **challenging** yoga practice?

What do I **know** that I'm not admitting?

What **strengths** did I use today?

weekly check - in

	09.00	13.00	17.00
	10.00	14.00	18.00
	11.00	15.00	19.00
	12.00	16.00	20.00

What have I achieved this week?

What's working with my practice and why is it working?

What's not working and what am I willing to do to upgrade it?

What is one thing I can do this week that will create the biggest results in my life?

What do I need to make a decision about?

How can I be more authentic?

What beliefs are holding me back and how can I upgrade them?

How can I open my chakras for more connection to my source?

Review Conscious Life Blueprin

Review Purpose Statement

Update 90-Day Planner

Add Actions to Weekly Planne

Plan Your Week

Old Habit >

New Habit >

New Actions >

New Affirmation/Mantra/Yoga Pos

weekly planner

1　　　　**2**　　　　**3**　　　　**4**

Projects & Appointments For This Week	Target date	Actions & Yoga Practice For This Week	Target date
monday			
tuesday			
wednesday			
thursday			
friday			
saturday			
sunday			

date:

creative space

My Yoga Practice

What I **love** about my work is...

Today I am inspired to take these **actions**:

	Meditation		Inspiration
	Yoga Practice		....

I have a **beautiful** mind and...

I AM

I AM

I AM

What did I **learn** on the yoga mat today?

How was my **mindset** today?

What new **habit** do I want to adopt into my life?

Where am I at this very moment?

6.00
7.00
8.00
9.00
10.00
11.00
12.00
13.00
14.00
15.00
16.00
17.00
18.00
19.00

My Yoga Practice

dream space

date:

I am so grateful for simple things like...

Meditation   Inspiration

Yoga Practice   . . . .

What is the best course of action to take today?

6.00

7.00

Today I am creative and...

8.00

I AM

I AM

9.00

I AM

10.00

Who AM I?

11.00

12.00

What am I supposed to do right now?

13.00

14.00

15.00

What new mindset do I want to adopt into my life?

16.00

17.00

How did my yoga practice feel today?

18.00

19.00

date:

soul space

My Yoga Practice

Today I am so **grateful** for...

My top 3 **inspired actions** for today are...

My **intentions** for today are...

I AM
I AM
I AM

What did I notice about my **yoga** practice today?

What did I **learn** today?

After today, what **behaviour** do I want to upgrade?

What **strengths** did I use today?

| Meditation | Inspiration |
| Yoga Practice | .... |

6.00

7.00

8.00

9.00

10.00

11.00

12.00

13.00

14.00

15.00

16.00

17.00

18.00

19.00

I AM awakening to my potential

date:

My Appreciation & gratitude list

Meditation   Inspiration

Yoga Practice   ....

Today, I am most inspired to do...

6.00

7.00

The mindset I wish to create today is...

I AM

I AM

8.00

I AM

9.00

10.00

What did I enjoy about today?

11.00

12.00

What challenged me today that I can learn from?

13.00

14.00

What new yoga pose would I like to perfect?

15.00

16.00

17.00

What did I do really well today?

18.00

19.00

date:

creative space

The things I am **grateful** for in my life are...

Today, I would **love** to do:

Today **i am focusing** on being...

I AM

I AM

I AM

What did I notice about my **thoughts** today?

What could I have handled **differently** today?

How can I open to **new** possibilities?

What am I **proud** of that came about today?

My Yoga Practice

| ■ Meditation | ■ Inspiration |
| ■ Yoga Practice | ■ .... |

6.00

7.00

8.00

9.00

10.00

11.00

12.00

13.00

14.00

15.00

16.00

17.00

18.00

19.00

date:

gratitude is Wisdom...

	Meditation		Inspiration
	Yoga Practice		....

6.00

7.00

8.00

9.00

10.00

11.00

12.00

13.00

14.00

15.00

16.00

17.00

18.00

19.00

Today, I feel **inspired** to do...

I create my day with my **thoughts**, therefore...

I AM

I AM

I AM

What did I **love** about my yoga practice today?

In what ways would I like to **grow**?

What would I like to **let go** of?

What was my underlying **motivation** today?

weekly check - in

	09.00	13.00	17.00
	10.00	14.00	18.00
	11.00	15.00	19.00
	12.00	16.00	20.00

What projects have I completed this week?

What's going well with my practice and why is it?

What do I find most challenging in my life right now?

What is one thing I can do this week that will create the biggest results in my life?

What am I happy about right now?

How can I be more empowered in my thoughts, words and actions?

What fears are holding me back and how can I overcome those?

How does my body feel? Am I feeling grounded?

Review Conscious Life Blueprint

Review Purpose Statement

Update 90-Day Planner

Add Actions to Weekly Planner

Plan Your Week

Old Habit >

New Habit >

New Actions >

New Affirmation/Mantra/Yoga Pose

weekly planner

4 Major Goals I'm Focused On This Week:

1   **2**   **3**   **4**

Projects & Appointments For This Week	Target date	Actions & Yoga Practice For This Week	Target date
monday			
tuesday			
wednesday			
thursday			
friday			
saturday			
sunday			

date:

soul space

My Yoga Practice

When I am **grateful** I open up to more...

| Meditation | Inspiration |
| Yoga Practice | .... |

What would I do **today**, if it was my last?

6.00

7.00

Today...

I AM

I AM

I AM

8.00

9.00

What was **interesting** about today?

10.00

11.00

12.00

What am I not **seeing**?

13.00

14.00

What ideas would I like to **upgrade**?

15.00

16.00

17.00

When was I completely in the **moment** today?

18.00

19.00

date:

Meditation   Inspiration

Yoga Practice   ....

6.00

7.00

8.00

9.00

10.00

11.00

12.00

13.00

14.00

15.00

16.00

17.00

18.00

19.00

Today, I give **thanks** for...

My **inspired** actions for today are...

Today I **honour** how I feel and...

I AM

I AM

I AM

What was today's **lesson**?

How can I create a more **challenging** yoga practice?

What do I **know** that I'm not admitting?

What **strengths** did I use today?

date:

creative space

What I **love** about my work is...

Today I am inspired to take these **actions:**

I have a **beautiful** mind and...

I AM

I AM

I AM

What did I **learn** on the yoga mat today?

How was my **mindset** today?

What new **habit** do I want to adopt into my life?

Where am I at this very moment?

Meditation   Inspiration

Yoga Practice   ....

6.00	
7.00	
8.00	
9.00	
10.00	
11.00	
12.00	
13.00	
14.00	
15.00	
16.00	
17.00	
18.00	
19.00	

I AM connected to my divine essence

My Yoga Practice

dream space

date:

- Meditation
- Inspiration
- Yoga Practice
- ....

6.00

7.00

8.00

9.00

10.00

11.00

12.00

13.00

14.00

15.00

16.00

17.00

18.00

19.00

I am so grateful for **simple** things like...

What is the best course of **action** to take today?

Today I **am** creative and...

I AM

I AM

I AM

Who AM I?

What am I supposed to do right **now**?

What new **mindset** do I want to adopt into my life?

How did my **yoga** practice feel today?

date:

soul space

Today I am so **grateful** for...

My top 3 **inspired actions** for today are...

■	Meditation	■	Inspiration
■	Yoga Practice	■	....

My **intentions** for today are...

I AM

I AM

I AM

What did I notice about my **yoga** practice today?

What did I **learn** today?

After today, what **behaviour** do I want to upgrade?

What **strengths** did I use today?

6.00
7.00
8.00
9.00
10.00
11.00
12.00
13.00
14.00
15.00
16.00
17.00
18.00
19.00

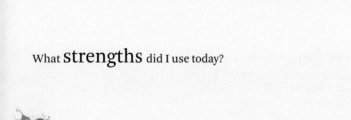

date:

My Appreciation & gratitude list

Meditation   Inspiration

Yoga Practice   ....

6.00

7.00

Today, I am most inspired to do...

8.00

9.00

The mindset I wish to create today is...

I AM

I AM

I AM

10.00

What did I enjoy about today?

11.00

12.00

What challenged me today that I can learn from?

13.00

14.00

15.00

What new yoga pose would I like to perfect?

16.00

17.00

What did I do really well today?

18.00

19.00

weekly check - in

	09.00	13.00	17.00
	10.00	14.00	18.00
	11.00	15.00	19.00
	12.00	16.00	20.00

What have I achieved on my Conscious Life Blueprint this week?

What do I need to start or stop?

In my relationships, how can I communicate better?

What is one thing I can do this week that will create the biggest results in my life?

What am I proud about right now?

How can I be happier and more grateful?

What negative attitudes are holding me back and how can I overcome those?

How can I stretch myself further in my yoga practice?

Review Conscious Life Blueprint

Review Purpose Statement

Update 90-Day Planner

Add Actions to Weekly Planner

Plan Your Week

Old Habit >

New Habit >

New Actions >

New Affirmation/Mantra/Yoga Pose

weekly planner

1	2	3	4

Projects & Appointments For This Week	Target date	Actions & Yoga Practice For This Week	Target date
monday			
tuesday			
wednesday			
thursday			
friday			
saturday			
sunday			

date:

creative space

The things I am **grateful** for in my life are...

Meditation   Inspiration

Yoga Practice   ....

Today, I would **love** to do:

| 6.00 |

| 7.00 |

Today **i am focusing** on being...

| 8.00 |

I AM

I AM

| 9.00 |

I AM

| 10.00 |

What did I notice about my **thoughts** today?

| 11.00 |

| 12.00 |

What could I have handled **differently** today?

| 13.00 |

| 14.00 |

How can I open to **new** possibilities?

| 15.00 |

| 16.00 |

| 17.00 |

What am I **proud** of that came about today?

| 18.00 |

| 19.00 |

gratitude is Wisdom...

Meditation   Inspiration

Yoga Practice   ·················

6.00

7.00

8.00

9.00

10.00

11.00

12.00

13.00

14.00

15.00

16.00

17.00

18.00

19.00

Today, I feel inspired to do...

I create my day with my thoughts, therefore...

I AM

I AM

I AM

What did I love about my yoga practice today?

In what ways would I like to grow?

What would I like to let go of?

What was my underlying motivation today?

date:

soul space
_____
_____
_____
_____
_____

My Yoga Practice
_____
_____
_____
_____
_____
_____
_____

When I am **grateful** I open up to more...

■ Meditation   ■ Inspiration

■ Yoga Practice   ■ ....

What would I do **today**, if it was my last?

6.00
7.00
8.00

Today...

I AM

I AM

I AM

I AM
pure
awareness

9.00

What was **interesting** about today?

10.00
11.00
12.00

What am I not **seeing**?

13.00
14.00

What ideas would I like to **upgrade**?

15.00
16.00
17.00

When was I completely in the **moment** today?

18.00
19.00

heart space

date:

Today, I give **thanks** for...

Meditation   Inspiration

Yoga Practice   ....

6.00

7.00

My **inspired** actions for today are...

8.00

Today I **honour** how I feel and...

I AM

I AM

9.00

I AM

10.00

What was today's **lesson**?

11.00

12.00

How can I create a more **challenging** yoga practice?

13.00

14.00

What do I **know** that I'm not admitting?

15.00

16.00

17.00

What **strengths** did I use today?

18.00

19.00

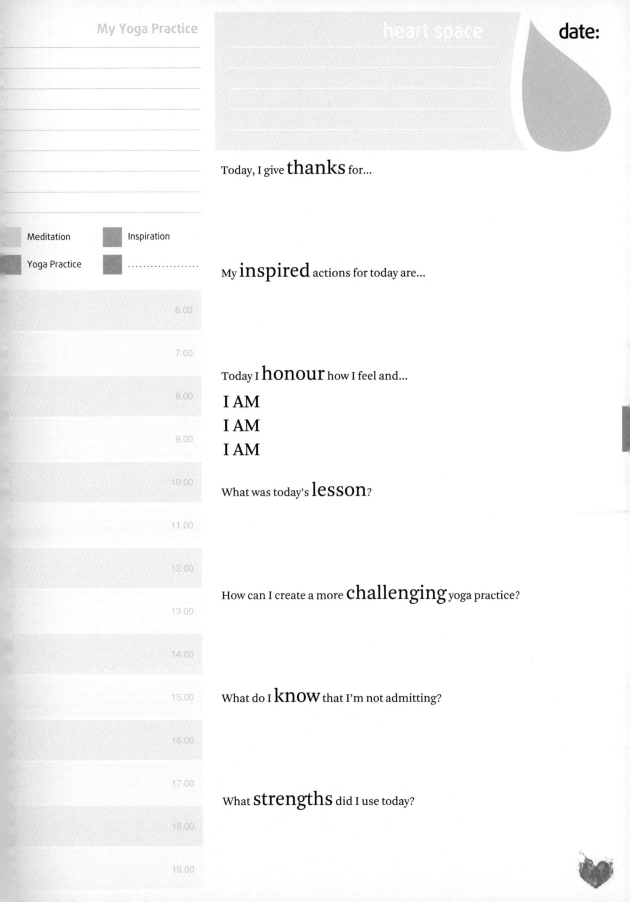

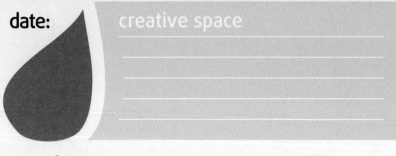

date:

creative space

My Yoga Practice

What I **love** about my work is...

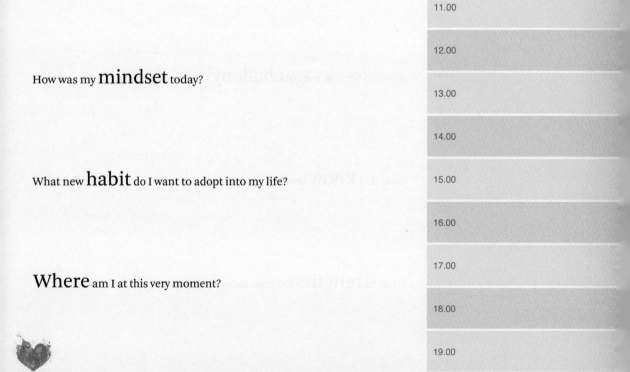

Today I am inspired to take these **actions**:

I have a **beautiful** mind and...

I AM

I AM

I AM

What did I **learn** on the yoga mat today?

How was my **mindset** today?

What new **habit** do I want to adopt into my life?

Where am I at this very moment?

| Meditation | Inspiration |
| Yoga Practice | .... |

6.00

7.00

8.00

9.00

10.00

11.00

12.00

13.00

14.00

15.00

16.00

17.00

18.00

19.00

dream space

date:

I am so grateful for **simple** things like...

Meditation   ☐ Inspiration

Yoga Practice   ☐ ....

6.00

7.00

What is the best course of **action** to take today?

8.00

9.00

Today I **am** creative and...

I AM

I AM

I AM

10.00

Who AM I?

11.00

12.00

What am I supposed to do right **now**?

13.00

14.00

15.00

What new **mindset** do I want to adopt into my life?

16.00

17.00

How did my **yoga** practice feel today?

18.00

19.00

weekly check - in

	09.00	13.00	17.00
	10.00	14.00	18.00
	11.00	15.00	19.00
	12.00	16.00	20.00

What major goals have I achieved this month?

How can I be more congruent with my thoughts, words and actions?

What are the biggest distractions to my yoga practice and how can I remove them?

What is one thing I can do this week that will create the biggest results in my life?

What am I committed to in my life right now?

How can I shine my light more?

What disempowering thoughts are holding me back and how can I upgrade those?

What new pose or asana can I incorporate into my current yoga practice?

Review Conscious Life Blueprin

Review Purpose Statement

Update 90-Day Planner

Add Actions to Weekly Planne

Plan Your Week

Old Habit >

New Habit >

New Actions >

New Affirmation/Mantra/Yoga Pos

weekly planner

4 Major Goals I'm Focused On This Week:

1 **2** **3** **4**

Projects & Appointments For This Week	Target date	Actions & Yoga Practice For This Week	Target date
monday			
tuesday			
wednesday			
thursday			
friday			
saturday			
sunday			

date:

soul space

My Yoga Practice

Today I am so **grateful** for...

	Meditation		Inspiration
	Yoga Practice		....

My top 3 **inspired actions** for today are...

My **intentions** for today are...

I AM

I AM

I AM

What did I notice about my **yoga** practice today?

What did I **learn** today?

After today, what **behaviour** do I want to upgrade?

What **strengths** did I use today?

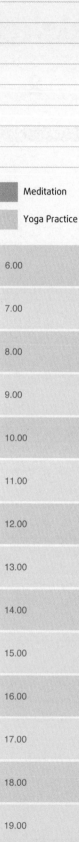

6.00

7.00

8.00

9.00

10.00

11.00

12.00

13.00

14.00

15.00

16.00

17.00

18.00

19.00

date:

My Appreciation & gratitude list

Meditation   Inspiration

Yoga Practice   . . . .

6.00

Today, I am most inspired to do...

7.00

8.00   The mindset I wish to create today is...

I AM

I AM
9.00
I AM

10.00   What did I enjoy about today?

11.00

12.00

13.00   What challenged me today that I can learn from?

14.00

15.00   What new yoga pose would I like to perfect?

16.00

17.00   What did I do really well today?

18.00

19.00

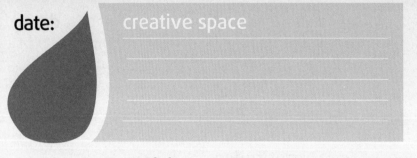

date:

creative space

My Yoga Practice

The things I am **grateful** for in my life are...

Today, I would **love** to do:

Today **i am focusing** on being...

I AM

I AM

I AM

What did I notice about my **thoughts** today?

What could I have handled **differently** today?

How can I open to **new** possibilities?

What am I **proud** of that came about today?

■ Meditation	■ Inspiration
■ Yoga Practice	■ ....

6.00

7.00

8.00

9.00

10.00

11.00

12.00

13.00

14.00

15.00

16.00

17.00

18.00

19.00

date:

gratitude is Wisdom...

Meditation   Inspiration

Yoga Practice   ....

Today, I feel **inspired** to do...

6.00

7.00

I create my day with my **thoughts**, therefore...

I AM

I AM

8.00

I AM

9.00

What did I **love** about my yoga practice today?

10.00

11.00

12.00

In what ways would I like to **grow**?

13.00

14.00

What would I like to **let go** of?

15.00

16.00

17.00

What was my underlying **motivation** today?

18.00

19.00

date:

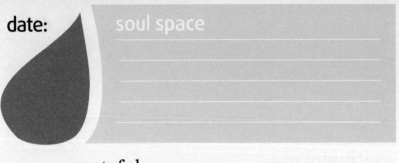

soul space

My Yoga Practice

When I am **grateful** I open up to more...

What would I do **today**, if it was my last?

I AM present

Today...
I AM
I AM
I AM

What was **interesting** about today?

What am I not **seeing**?

What ideas would I like to **upgrade**?

When was I completely in the **moment** today?

6.00	
7.00	
8.00	
9.00	
10.00	
11.00	
12.00	
13.00	
14.00	
15.00	
16.00	
17.00	
18.00	
19.00	

date:

Meditation

Inspiration

Yoga Practice

....

6.00

7.00

8.00

9.00

10.00

11.00

12.00

13.00

14.00

15.00

16.00

17.00

18.00

19.00

Today, I give **thanks** for...

My **inspired** actions for today are...

Today I **honour** how I feel and...

I AM

I AM

I AM

What was today's **lesson**?

How can I create a more **challenging** yoga practice?

What do I **know** that I'm not admitting?

What **strengths** did I use today?

weekly check - in

	09.00	13.00	17.00
	10.00	14.00	18.00
	11.00	15.00	19.00
	12.00	16.00	20.00

What have I achieved this week?

☐ Review Conscious Life Blueprin

☐ Review Purpose Statement

What's working with my practice and why is it working?

☐ Update 90-Day Planner

☐ Add Actions to Weekly Planne

☐ Plan Your Week

What's not working and what am I willing to do to upgrade it?

Old Habit >

What is one thing I can do this week that will create the biggest results in my life?

New Habit >

What do I need to make a decision about?

How can I be more authentic?

New Actions >

What beliefs are holding me back and how can I upgrade them?

New Affirmation/Mantra/Yoga Po

How can I open my chakras for more connection to my source?

weekly planner

1

2

3

4

Projects & Appointments For This Week	Target date	Actions & Yoga Practice For This Week	Target date

monday

tuesday

wednesday

thursday

friday

saturday

sunday

date: creative space

My Yoga Practice

What I **love** about my work is...

Today I am inspired to take these **actions**:

| | Meditation | | Inspiration |
| | Yoga Practice | | .... |

I have a **beautiful** mind and...

I AM
I AM
I AM

What did I **learn** on the yoga mat today?

How was my **mindset** today?

What new **habit** do I want to adopt into my life?

Where am I at this very moment?

| 6.00 |
| 7.00 |
| 8.00 |
| 9.00 |
| 10.00 |
| 11.00 |
| 12.00 |
| 13.00 |
| 14.00 |
| 15.00 |
| 16.00 |
| 17.00 |
| 18.00 |
| 19.00 |

dream space

date:

I am so grateful for **simple** things like...

Meditation   Inspiration

Yoga Practice   ....

6.00

7.00

What is the best course of **action** to take today?

8.00

9.00

Today I **am** creative and...

I AM

I AM

I AM

10.00

Who AM I?

11.00

12.00

What am I supposed to do right **now**?

13.00

14.00

What new **mindset** do I want to adopt into my life?

15.00

16.00

17.00

How did my **yoga** practice feel today?

18.00

19.00

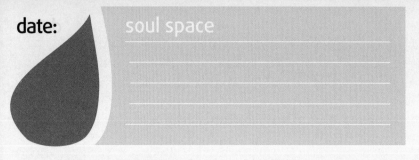

date:

soul space

Today I am so **grateful** for...

My top 3 **inspired actions** for today are...

My **intentions** for today are...

I AM

I AM

I AM

What did I notice about my **yoga** practice today?

What did I **learn** today?

After today, what **behaviour** do I want to upgrade?

What **strengths** did I use today?

My Yoga Practice

Meditation   Inspiration

Yoga Practice   ....

| 6.00 |
| 7.00 |
| 8.00 |
| 9.00 |
| 10.00 |
| 11.00 |
| 12.00 |
| 13.00 |
| 14.00 |
| 15.00 |
| 16.00 |
| 17.00 |
| 18.00 |
| 19.00 |

date:

My Appreciation & gratitude list

Meditation   Inspiration

Yoga Practice   ....

Today, I am most inspired to do...

6.00

7.00

The mindset I wish to create today is...

I AM

I AM

8.00

I AM

9.00

What did I enjoy about today?

10.00

11.00

12.00

What challenged me today that I can learn from?

13.00

14.00

15.00

What new yoga pose would I like to perfect?

16.00

17.00

What did I do really well today?

18.00

19.00

date:

creative space

My Yoga Practice

The things I am **grateful** for in my life are...

Today, I would **love** to do:

Today **i am focusing** on being...

I AM

I AM

I AM

What did I notice about my **thoughts** today?

What could I have handled **differently** today?

How can I open to **new** possibilities?

What am I **proud** of that came about today?

	Meditation		Inspiration
	Yoga Practice		....

| 6.00 |
| 7.00 |
| 8.00 |
| 9.00 |
| 10.00 |
| 11.00 |
| 12.00 |
| 13.00 |
| 14.00 |
| 15.00 |
| 16.00 |
| 17.00 |
| 18.00 |
| 19.00 |

dream space

date:

gratitude is Wisdom...

Meditation   Inspiration

Yoga Practice   ....

6.00

7.00

Today, I feel **inspired** to do...

8.00

9.00

I create my day with my **thoughts**, therefore...

I AM

I AM

I AM

10.00

What did I **love** about my yoga practice today?

11.00

12.00

In what ways would I like to **grow**?

13.00

14.00

I AM
conscious

15.00

What would I like to **let go** of?

16.00

17.00

What was my underlying **motivation** today?

18.00

19.00

weekly check - in

	09.00	13.00	17.00
	10.00	14.00	18.00
	11.00	15.00	19.00
	12.00	16.00	20.00

What projects have I completed this week?

☐ Review Conscious Life Blueprint

☐ Review Purpose Statement

What's going well with my practice and why is it?

☐ Update 90-Day Planner

☐ Add Actions to Weekly Planner

☐ Plan Your Week

What do I find most challenging in my life right now?

Old Habit >

What is one thing I can do this week that will create the biggest results in my life?

New Habit >

What am I happy about right now?

How can I be more empowered in my thoughts, words and actions?

New Actions >

What fears are holding me back and how can I overcome those?

New Affirmation/Mantra/Yoga Pose

How does my body feel? Am I feeling grounded?

4 Major Goals I'm Focused On This Week:

1	2	3	4

Projects & Appointments For This Week	Target date	Actions & Yoga Practice For This Week	Target date
monday			
tuesday			
wednesday			
thursday			
friday			
saturday			
sunday			

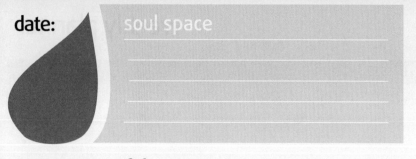

date:

soul space

My Yoga Practice

When I am **grateful** I open up to more...

| ▇ Meditation | ▇ Inspiration |
| ▇ Yoga Practice | ▇ .... |

What would I do **today**, if it was my last?

6.00
7.00

Today...

I AM

I AM

8.00

I AM

9.00

What was **interesting** about today?

10.00
11.00
12.00

What am I not **seeing**?

13.00
14.00

What ideas would I like to **upgrade**?

15.00
16.00
17.00

When was I completely in the **moment** today?

18.00
19.00

date:

Meditation   Inspiration

Yoga Practice   ....

6.00

7.00

8.00

9.00

10.00

11.00

12.00

13.00

14.00

15.00

16.00

17.00

18.00

19.00

Today, I give **thanks** for...

My **inspired** actions for today are...

Today I **honour** how I feel and...

I AM

I AM

I AM

What was today's **lesson**?

How can I create a more **challenging** yoga practice?

What do I **know** that I'm not admitting?

I AM
happy,
healthy &
connected

What **strengths** did I use today?

date:

creative space

My Yoga Practice

What I **love** about my work is...

Today I am inspired to take these **actions**:

■ Meditation		■ Inspiration	
■ Yoga Practice		■	

I have a **beautiful** mind and...

I AM

I AM

I AM

What did I **learn** on the yoga mat today?

How was my **mindset** today?

What new **habit** do I want to adopt into my life?

Where am I at this very moment?

6.00

7.00

8.00

9.00

10.00

11.00

12.00

13.00

14.00

15.00

16.00

17.00

18.00

19.00

date:

I am so grateful for simple things like...

Meditation   Inspiration

Yoga Practice   ....

6.00

7.00

8.00

9.00

10.00

11.00

12.00

13.00

14.00

15.00

16.00

17.00

18.00

19.00

What is the best course of action to take today?

Today I am creative and...

I AM

I AM

I AM

Who AM I?

What am I supposed to do right now?

What new mindset do I want to adopt into my life?

How did my yoga practice feel today?

date:

soul space

Today I am so **grateful** for...

My top 3 **inspired actions** for today are...

My **intentions** for today are...

I AM

I AM

I AM

What did I notice about my **yoga** practice today?

What did I **learn** today?

After today, what **behaviour** do I want to upgrade?

What **strengths** did I use today?

Meditation   Inspiration

Yoga Practice   ....

6.00	
7.00	
8.00	
9.00	
10.00	
11.00	
12.00	
13.00	
14.00	
15.00	
16.00	
17.00	
18.00	
19.00	

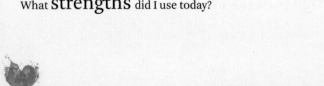

date:

_____
_____
_____
_____
_____
_____
_____
_____

My Appreciation & gratitude list

▢ Meditation   ▢ Inspiration

▢ Yoga Practice   ▢ ················

Today, I am most inspired to do...

6.00

7.00

The mindset I wish to create today is...

8.00

I AM

I AM

9.00

I AM

10.00

What did I enjoy about today?

11.00

12.00

What challenged me today that I can learn from?

13.00

14.00

15.00

What new yoga pose would I like to perfect?

16.00

17.00

What did I do really well today?

18.00

19.00

weekly check - in

	09.00	13.00	17.00
	10.00	14.00	18.00
	11.00	15.00	19.00
	12.00	16.00	20.00

What have I achieved on my Conscious Life Blueprint this week?

What do I need to start or stop?

In my relationships, how can I communicate better?

What is one thing I can do this week that will create the biggest results in my life?

What am I proud about right now?

How can I be happier and more grateful?

What negative attitudes are holding me back and how can I overcome those?

How can I stretch myself further in my yoga practice?

Review Conscious Life Blueprint

Review Purpose Statement

Update 90-Day Planner

Add Actions to Weekly Planner

Plan Your Week

Old Habit >

New Habit >

New Actions >

New Affirmation/Mantra/Yoga Pos

weekly planner

1	2	3	4

Projects & Appointments For This Week	Target date	Actions & Yoga Practice For This Week	Target date
monday			
tuesday			
wednesday			
thursday			
friday			
saturday			
sunday			

date:

creative space

The things I am **grateful** for in my life are...

Today, I would **love** to do:

Today **i am focusing** on being...

I AM

I AM

I AM

What did I notice about my **thoughts** today?

What could I have handled **differently** today?

How can I open to **new** possibilities?

What am I **proud** of that came about today?

My Yoga Practice

■ Meditation	■ Inspiration
■ Yoga Practice	■ ....

6.00

7.00

8.00

9.00

10.00

11.00

12.00

13.00

14.00

15.00

16.00

17.00

18.00

19.00

date:

Meditation   Inspiration

Yoga Practice   ....

6.00

7.00

8.00

9.00

10.00

11.00

12.00

13.00

14.00

15.00

16.00

17.00

18.00

19.00

gratitude is Wisdom...

Today, I feel **inspired** to do...

I create my day with my **thoughts**, therefore...

I AM

I AM

I AM

What did I **love** about my yoga practice today?

In what ways would I like to **grow**?

What would I like to **let go** of?

What was my underlying **motivation** today?

date:

soul space

My Yoga Practice

When I am **grateful** I open up to more...

What would I do **today**, if it was my last?

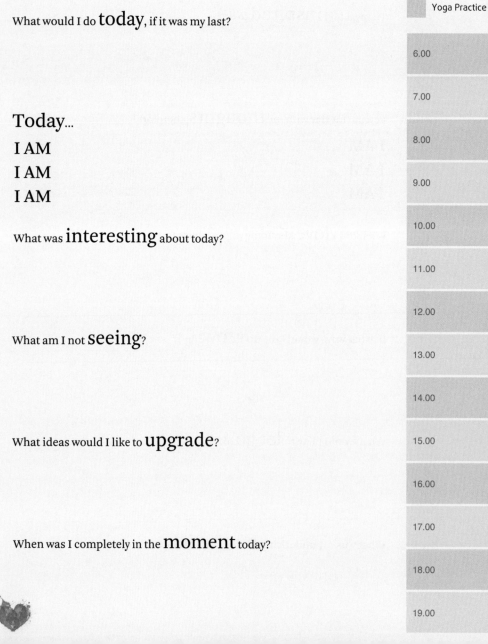

| Meditation | Inspiration |
| Yoga Practice | .... |

Today...

I AM

I AM

I AM

What was **interesting** about today?

What am I not **seeing**?

What ideas would I like to **upgrade**?

When was I completely in the **moment** today?

| 6.00 |
| 7.00 |
| 8.00 |
| 9.00 |
| 10.00 |
| 11.00 |
| 12.00 |
| 13.00 |
| 14.00 |
| 15.00 |
| 16.00 |
| 17.00 |
| 18.00 |
| 19.00 |

date:

Meditation

Inspiration

Yoga Practice

....

6.00

7.00

8.00

9.00

10.00

11.00

12.00

13.00

14.00

15.00

16.00

17.00

18.00

19.00

Today, I give **thanks** for...

My **inspired** actions for today are...

Today I **honour** how I feel and...

I AM

I AM

I AM

What was today's **lesson**?

How can I create a more **challenging** yoga practice?

What do I **know** that I'm not admitting?

What **strengths** did I use today?

I AM
empowered

date:

creative space

My Yoga Practice

What I **love** about my work is...

Today I am inspired to take these **actions**:

■ Meditation   ■ Inspiration

■ Yoga Practice   ■ ....

I have a **beautiful** mind and...

I AM

I AM

I AM

What did I **learn** on the yoga mat today?

How was my **mindset** today?

What new **habit** do I want to adopt into my life?

Where am I at this very moment?

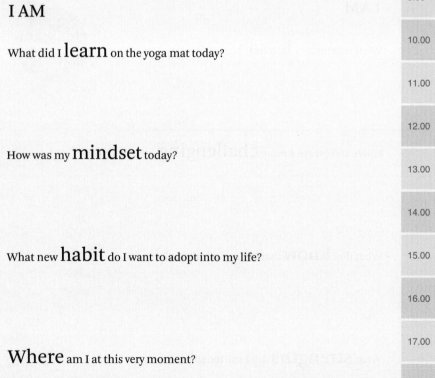

Time
6.00
7.00
8.00
9.00
10.00
11.00
12.00
13.00
14.00
15.00
16.00
17.00
18.00
19.00

date:

I am so grateful for simple things like...

Meditation   Inspiration

Yoga Practice   ....

What is the best course of action to take today?

6.00

7.00

Today I am creative and...

I AM

I AM

I AM

8.00

9.00

10.00

Who AM I?

11.00

12.00

What am I supposed to do right now?

13.00

14.00

What new mindset do I want to adopt into my life?

15.00

16.00

17.00

How did my yoga practice feel today?

18.00

19.00

weekly check - in

	09.00	13.00	17.00
	10.00	14.00	18.00
	11.00	15.00	19.00
	12.00	16.00	20.00

What major goals have I achieved this month?

How can I be more congruent with my thoughts, words and actions?

What are the biggest distractions to my yoga practice and how can I remove them?

What is one thing I can do this week that will create the biggest results in my life?

What am I committed to in my life right now?

How can I shine my light more?

What disempowering thoughts are holding me back and how can I upgrade those?

What new pose or asana can I incorporate into my current yoga practice?

☐ Review Conscious Life Blueprin

☐ Review Purpose Statement

☐ Update 90-Day Planner

☐ Add Actions to Weekly Planne

☐ Plan Your Week

Old Habit >

New Habit >

New Actions >

New Affirmation/Mantra/Yoga Po

weekly planner

4 Major Goals I'm Focused On This Week:

1	2	3	4

Projects & Appointments For This Week	Target date	Actions & Yoga Practice For This Week	Target date
monday			
tuesday			
wednesday			
thursday			
friday			
saturday			
sunday			

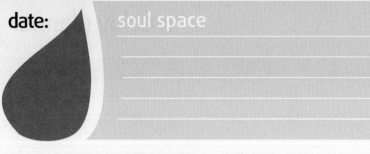

date:

soul space

Today I am so grateful for...

My top 3 inspired actions for today are...

My intentions for today are...

I AM

I AM

I AM

What did I notice about my yoga practice today?

What did I learn today?

After today, what behaviour do I want to upgrade?

What strengths did I use today?

My Yoga Practice

■ Meditation   ■ Inspiration

■ Yoga Practice   ■ ....

6.00

7.00

8.00

9.00

10.00

11.00

12.00

13.00

14.00

15.00

16.00

17.00

18.00

19.00

date:

My Appreciation & gratitude list

Meditation   Inspiration

Yoga Practice   ....

Today, I am most inspired to do...

6.00

7.00

The mindset I wish to create today is...

I AM

I AM
8.00

I AM
9.00

What did I enjoy about today?

10.00

11.00

12.00

What challenged me today that I can learn from?

13.00

14.00

What new yoga pose would I like to perfect?
15.00

16.00

17.00

What did I do really well today?

18.00

19.00

date:

creative space

My Yoga Practice

The things I am **grateful** for in my life are...

Today, I would **love** to do:

Today **i am focusing** on being...

I AM

I AM

I AM

What did I notice about my **thoughts** today?

What could I have handled **differently** today?

How can I open to **new** possibilities?

What am I **proud** of that came about today?

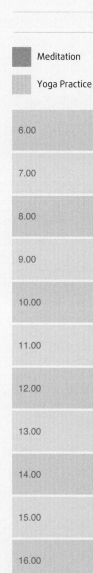

Meditation   Inspiration

Yoga Practice   ....

6.00

7.00

8.00

9.00

10.00

11.00

12.00

13.00

14.00

15.00

16.00

17.00

18.00

19.00

dream space

date:

Meditation   Inspiration

Yoga Practice   ....

6.00

7.00

8.00

9.00

10.00

11.00

12.00

13.00

14.00

15.00

16.00

17.00

18.00

19.00

gratitude is Wisdom...

Today, I feel **inspired** to do...

I create my day with my **thoughts**, therefore...

I AM

I AM

I AM

What did I **love** about my yoga practice today?

In what ways would I like to **grow**?

What would I like to **let go** of?

What was my underlying **motivation** today?

date:

soul space

My Yoga Practice

When I am grateful I open up to more...

| ☐ Meditation | ☐ Inspiration |
| ☐ Yoga Practice | ☐ .... |

What would I do today, if it was my last?

| 6.00 |
| 7.00 |

Today...

I AM

I AM

I AM

| 8.00 |
| 9.00 |

What was interesting about today?

| 10.00 |
| 11.00 |
| 12.00 |

What am I not seeing?

| 13.00 |
| 14.00 |

What ideas would I like to upgrade?

| 15.00 |
| 16.00 |
| 17.00 |

When was I completely in the moment today?

| 18.00 |
| 19.00 |

date:

Meditation | Inspiration

Yoga Practice | ....

6.00

7.00

8.00

9.00

10.00

11.00

12.00

13.00

14.00

15.00

16.00

17.00

18.00

19.00

Today, I give **thanks** for...

My **inspired** actions for today are...

I AM pure awareness

Today I **honour** how I feel and...

I AM

I AM

I AM

What was today's **lesson**?

How can I create a more **challenging** yoga practice?

What do I **know** that I'm not admitting?

What **strengths** did I use today?

weekly check - in

09.00	13.00	17.00
10.00	14.00	18.00
11.00	15.00	19.00
12.00	16.00	20.00

What have I achieved this week?

What's working with my practice and why is it working?

What's not working and what am I willing to do to upgrade it?

What is one thing I can do this week that will create the biggest results in my life?

What do I need to make a decision about?

How can I be more authentic?

What beliefs are holding me back and how can I upgrade them?

How can I open my chakras for more connection to my source?

Review Conscious Life Blueprin

Review Purpose Statement

Update 90-Day Planner

Add Actions to Weekly Planne

Plan Your Week

Old Habit >

New Habit >

New Actions >

New Affirmation/Mantra/Yoga Pos

weekly planner

| 1 | 2 | 3 | 4 |

Projects & Appointments For This Week	Target date	Actions & Yoga Practice For This Week	Target date

monday

tuesday

wednesday

thursday

friday

saturday

sunday

date:

creative space

What I **love** about my work is...

Meditation	Inspiration
Yoga Practice	....

Today I am inspired to take these **actions**:

I have a **beautiful** mind and...

I AM

I AM

I AM

What did I **learn** on the yoga mat today?

How was my **mindset** today?

What new **habit** do I want to adopt into my life?

Where am I at this very moment?

6.00	
7.00	
8.00	
9.00	
10.00	
11.00	
12.00	
13.00	
14.00	
15.00	
16.00	
17.00	
18.00	
19.00	

date:

I am so grateful for **simple** things like...

Meditation   Inspiration

Yoga Practice   ....

What is the best course of **action** to take today?

6.00

7.00

Today I **am** creative and...

8.00

I AM

I AM

9.00

I AM

10.00

Who AM I?

11.00

12.00

What am I supposed to do right **now**?

13.00

14.00

15.00

What new **mindset** do I want to adopt into my life?

16.00

17.00

How did my **yoga** practice feel today?

18.00

19.00

date:

soul space

My Yoga Practice

Today I am so **grateful** for...

Meditation		Inspiration
Yoga Practice		....

My top 3 **inspired actions** for today are...

My **intentions** for today are...

I AM

I AM

I AM

What did I notice about my **yoga** practice today?

What did I **learn** today?

After today, what **behaviour** do I want to upgrade?

What **strengths** did I use today?

6.00

7.00

8.00

9.00

10.00

11.00

12.00

13.00

14.00

15.00

16.00

17.00

18.00

19.00

date:

My Appreciation & gratitude list

Meditation   Inspiration

Yoga Practice   ....

6.00

Today, I am most inspired to do...

7.00

8.00

The mindset I wish to create today is...

I AM

I AM

9.00

I AM

10.00

What did I enjoy about today?

11.00

12.00

What challenged me today that I can learn from?

I AM connected to my divine essence

13.00

14.00

What new yoga pose would I like to perfect?

15.00

16.00

17.00

What did I do really well today?

18.00

19.00

date:

creative space

My Yoga Practice

The things I am **grateful** for in my life are...

	Meditation		Inspiration
	Yoga Practice		....

Today, I would **love** to do:

6.00	
7.00	

Today **i am focusing** on being...

I AM

I AM

I AM

8.00	
9.00	
10.00	

What did I notice about my **thoughts** today?

11.00	
12.00	

What could I have handled **differently** today?

13.00	
14.00	

How can I open to **new** possibilities?

15.00	
16.00	
17.00	

What am I **proud** of that came about today?

18.00	
19.00	

date:

gratitude is Wisdom...

Meditation   Inspiration

Yoga Practice   ....

Today, I feel inspired to do...

6.00

7.00

I create my day with my thoughts, therefore...

8.00

I AM

I AM

9.00

I AM

10.00

What did I love about my yoga practice today?

11.00

12.00

In what ways would I like to grow?

13.00

14.00

15.00   What would I like to let go of?

16.00

17.00

What was my underlying motivation today?

18.00

19.00

weekly check - in

	09.00	13.00	17.00
	10.00	14.00	18.00
	11.00	15.00	19.00
	12.00	16.00	20.00

What projects have I completed this week?

What's going well with my practice and why is it?

What do I find most challenging in my life right now?

What is one thing I can do this week that will create the biggest results in my life?

What am I happy about right now?

How can I be more empowered in my thoughts, words and actions?

What fears are holding me back and how can I overcome those?

How does my body feel? Am I feeling grounded?

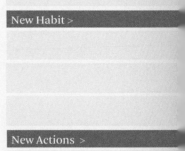

Review Conscious Life Blueprir

Review Purpose Statement

Update 90-Day Planner

Add Actions to Weekly Planne

Plan Your Week

Old Habit >

New Habit >

New Actions >

New Affirmation/Mantra/Yoga Po:

weekly planner

4 Major Goals I'm Focused On This Week:

1	2	3	4

Projects & Appointments For This Week	Target date	Actions & Yoga Practice For This Week	Target date
monday			
tuesday			
wednesday			
thursday			
friday			
saturday			
sunday			

date:

soul space

My Yoga Practice

When I am **grateful** I open up to more...

What would I do **today**, if it was my last?

| Meditation | Inspiration |
| Yoga Practice | .... |

Today...

I AM

I AM

I AM

I AM empowered

What was **interesting** about today?

What am I not **seeing**?

What ideas would I like to **upgrade**?

When was I completely in the **moment** today?

6.00

7.00

8.00

9.00

10.00

11.00

12.00

13.00

14.00

15.00

16.00

17.00

18.00

19.00

Today, I give **thanks** for...

Meditation   Inspiration

Yoga Practice   ....

6.00

7.00

My **inspired** actions for today are...

8.00

Today I **honour** how I feel and...

I AM

I AM

9.00

I AM

10.00

What was today's **lesson**?

11.00

12.00

How can I create a more **challenging** yoga practice?

13.00

14.00

15.00

What do I **know** that I'm not admitting?

16.00

17.00

What **strengths** did I use today?

18.00

19.00

date:

My Yoga Practice

What I **love** about my work is...

Today I am inspired to take these **actions**:

6.00	
7.00	
8.00	
9.00	

I have a **beautiful** mind and...

I AM
I AM
I AM

10.00	
11.00	

What did I **learn** on the yoga mat today?

12.00	
13.00	

How was my **mindset** today?

14.00	
15.00	

What new **habit** do I want to adopt into my life?

16.00	
17.00	

Where am I at this very moment?

18.00	
19.00	

date:

I am so grateful for **simple** things like...

Meditation   Inspiration

Yoga Practice   . . . .

6.00

7.00

What is the best course of **action** to take today?

8.00

9.00

Today I **am** creative and...

I AM

I AM

I AM

10.00

11.00

Who AM I?

12.00

13.00

What am I supposed to do right **now**?

14.00

15.00

What new **mindset** do I want to adopt into my life?

16.00

17.00

How did my **yoga** practice feel today?

18.00

19.00

date:

soul space

Today I am so **grateful** for...

My top 3 **inspired actions** for today are...

Meditation   Inspiration

Yoga Practice   ....

My **intentions** for today are...

I AM

I AM

I AM

What did I notice about my **yoga** practice today?

What did I **learn** today?

After today, what **behaviour** do I want to upgrade?

What **strengths** did I use today?

6.00	
7.00	
8.00	
9.00	
10.00	
11.00	
12.00	
13.00	
14.00	
15.00	
16.00	
17.00	
18.00	
19.00	

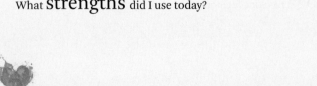

date:

My Appreciation & gratitude list

Meditation   Inspiration

Yoga Practice   ....

Today, I am most inspired to do...

6.00

7.00

The mindset I wish to create today is...

8.00

I AM

I AM

9.00

I AM

10.00

What did I enjoy about today?

11.00

12.00

What challenged me today that I can learn from?

13.00

14.00

What new yoga pose would I like to perfect?

15.00

16.00

17.00

What did I do really well today?

18.00

19.00

weekly check - in

	09.00	13.00	17.00
	10.00	14.00	18.00
	11.00	15.00	19.00
	12.00	16.00	20.00

What have I achieved on my Conscious Life Blueprint this week?

What do I need to start or stop?

In my relationships, how can I communicate better?

What is one thing I can do this week that will create the biggest results in my life?

What am I proud about right now?

How can I be happier and more grateful?

What negative attitudes are holding me back and how can I overcome those?

How can I stretch myself further in my yoga practice?

Review Conscious Life Blueprint

Review Purpose Statement

Update 90-Day Planner

Add Actions to Weekly Planner

Plan Your Week

Old Habit >

New Habit >

New Actions >

New Affirmation/Mantra/Yoga Pose

weekly planner

4 Major Goals I'm Focused On This Week:

1	2	3	4

Projects & Appointments For This Week	Target date	Actions & Yoga Practice For This Week	Target date
monday			
tuesday			
wednesday			
thursday			
friday			
saturday			
sunday			

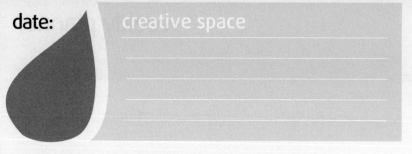

date:

creative space

My Yoga Practice

The things I am grateful for in my life are...

Today, I would love to do:

Today i am focusing on being...

I AM

I AM

I AM

What did I notice about my thoughts today?

What could I have handled differently today?

How can I open to new possibilities?

What am I proud of that came about today?

Meditation	Inspiration
Yoga Practice	....

6.00

7.00

8.00

9.00

10.00

11.00

12.00

13.00

14.00

15.00

16.00

17.00

18.00

19.00

dream space

date:

gratitude is Wisdom...

Meditation   Inspiration

Yoga Practice   ....

6.00

7.00

Today, I feel inspired to do...

8.00

9.00

I create my day with my thoughts, therefore...

I AM

I AM

I AM

10.00

What did I love about my yoga practice today?

11.00

12.00

In what ways would I like to grow?

13.00

14.00

15.00

What would I like to let go of?

16.00

17.00

What was my underlying motivation today?

18.00

19.00

date:

soul space

My Yoga Practice

When I am **grateful** I open up to more...

What would I do **today**, if it was my last?

Today...
I AM
I AM
I AM

What was **interesting** about today?

What am I not **seeing**?

What ideas would I like to **upgrade**?

When was I completely in the **moment** today?

	Meditation		Inspiration
	Yoga Practice		....

6.00
7.00
8.00
9.00
10.00
11.00
12.00
13.00
14.00
15.00
16.00
17.00
18.00
19.00

Today, I give **thanks** for...

Meditation   Inspiration

Yoga Practice   ....

6.00

7.00

My **inspired** actions for today are...

8.00

9.00

Today I **honour** how I feel and...

I AM

I AM

I AM

10.00

What was today's **lesson**?

11.00

12.00

How can I create a more **challenging** yoga practice?

13.00

14.00

15.00

What do I **know** that I'm not admitting?

16.00

17.00

What **strengths** did I use today?

18.00

19.00

date:

creative space

My Yoga Practice

What I **love** about my work is...

■ Meditation	■ Inspiration
■ Yoga Practice	■ ....

Today I am inspired to take these **actions:**

6.00

7.00

I have a **beautiful** mind and...

I AM
I AM
I AM

8.00

9.00

What did I **learn** on the yoga mat today?

10.00

11.00

12.00

How was my **mindset** today?

13.00

14.00

What new **habit** do I want to adopt into my life?

15.00

16.00

17.00

Where am I at this very moment?

18.00

19.00

date:

I am so grateful for **simple** things like...

Meditation   Inspiration

Yoga Practice   ....

What is the best course of **action** to take today?

6.00

7.00

Today I **am** creative and...

8.00

I AM

I AM

9.00

I AM

10.00

Who AM I?

11.00

12.00

What am I supposed to do right **now**?

13.00

14.00

15.00

What new **mindset** do I want to adopt into my life?

16.00

17.00

How did my **yoga** practice feel today?

18.00

19.00

weekly check - in

	09.00	13.00	17.00
	10.00	14.00	18.00
	11.00	15.00	19.00
	12.00	16.00	20.00

What major goals have I achieved this month?

How can I be more congruent with my thoughts, words and actions?

What are the biggest distractions to my yoga practice and how can I remove them?

What is one thing I can do this week that will create the biggest results in my life?

What am I committed to in my life right now?

How can I shine my light more?

What disempowering thoughts are holding me back and how can I upgrade those?

What new pose or asana can I incorporate into my current yoga practice?

Review Conscious Life Blueprin

Review Purpose Statement

Update 90-Day Planner

Add Actions to Weekly Planne

Plan Your Week

Old Habit >

New Habit >

New Actions >

 New Affirmation/Mantra/Yoga Pos

weekly planner

1	2	3	4

Projects & Appointments For This Week	Target date	Actions & Yoga Practice For This Week	Target date
monday			
tuesday			
wednesday			
thursday			
friday			
saturday			
sunday			

date:

soul space

My Yoga Practice

Today I am so **grateful** for...

Meditation	Inspiration
Yoga Practice	....

My top 3 **inspired actions** for today are...

6.00	

| 7.00 |

My **intentions** for today are...

I AM

I AM   8.00

I AM
                     9.00

What did I notice about my **yoga** practice today?

10.00

11.00

12.00

What did I **learn** today?
                     13.00

14.00

After today, what **behaviour** do I want to upgrade?   15.00

16.00

17.00

What **strengths** did I use today?

18.00

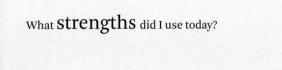

19.00

date:

My Appreciation & gratitude list

Meditation   Inspiration

Yoga Practice   ....

6.00

7.00

8.00

9.00

10.00

11.00

12.00

13.00

14.00

15.00

16.00

17.00

18.00

19.00

Today, I am most inspired to do...

The mindset I wish to create today is...

I AM

I AM

I AM

What did I enjoy about today?

What challenged me today that I can learn from?

What new yoga pose would I like to perfect?

What did I do really well today?

date:

creative space

My Yoga Practice

The things I am **grateful** for in my life are...

☐ Meditation	☐ Inspiration
☐ Yoga Practice	☐ ....

Today, I would **love** to do:

Today **i am focusing** on being...

I AM

I AM

I AM

What did I notice about my **thoughts** today?

What could I have handled **differently** today?

How can I open to **new** possibilities?

What am I **proud** of that came about today?

6.00

7.00

8.00

9.00

10.00

11.00

12.00

13.00

14.00

15.00

16.00

17.00

18.00

19.00

dream space

date:

Meditation   Inspiration

Yoga Practice   ....

6.00

7.00

8.00

9.00

10.00

11.00

12.00

13.00

14.00

15.00

16.00

17.00

18.00

19.00

gratitude is Wisdom...

Today, I feel inspired to do...

I create my day with my thoughts, therefore...

I AM

I AM

I AM

What did I love about my yoga practice today?

In what ways would I like to grow?

What would I like to let go of?

What was my underlying motivation today?

date:

soul space

My Yoga Practice

When I am **grateful** I open up to more...

| Meditation | | Inspiration |
| Yoga Practice | | .... |

What would I do **today**, if it was my last?

6.00

7.00

Today...
I AM
I AM
I AM

8.00

9.00

What was **interesting** about today?

10.00

11.00

12.00

What am I not **seeing**?

13.00

14.00

What ideas would I like to **upgrade**?

15.00

16.00

17.00

When was I completely in the **moment** today?

18.00

19.00

date:

Meditation   Inspiration

Yoga Practice   ·················

6.00

7.00

8.00

9.00

10.00

11.00

12.00

13.00

14.00

15.00

16.00

17.00

18.00

19.00

Today, I give **thanks** for...

My **inspired** actions for today are...

Today I **honour** how I feel and...

I AM

I AM

I AM

What was today's **lesson**?

How can I create a more **challenging** yoga practice?

What do I **know** that I'm not admitting?

What **strengths** did I use today?

90 day check-in

Welcome to your 90-day check-in! It's time to celebrate your achievements, identify what needs attention and reset your focus for the next 90 days. Use the answers to the following questions to plan your next quarter and to stay inspired and motivated towards your goals.

What major goals have I achieved this past 90 days?
What am I happy about?

Does my vision still inspire me or do I need to create a new one?
How can I be more aligned with my Conscious Life Blueprint?

What new potentials have I witnessed unfolding
in my life in the last 90 days?

What new mindset do I wish to develop?
What is no longer acceptable to me?

Am I embracing change or resisting it?
How can I open up to more inner expansion?

Am I honouring myself with enough self-love,
self-respect, self-care? How can I love myself more?
What do I need to say yes or no to?

What goal or project am I focusing on for the next 90 days?

What would I love to consciously create over the next 90 days?

Review Conscious Life Blueprint	Review Your Yearly Planner	Plan Your Week
Review Purpose Statement	Complete Next 90 Day Planner	Celebrate Your Progress!

Month:

Goal:

Target date:

Actions to complete this goal:

1.

2.

3.

4.

Why I'd love to achieve this goal:

How will I feel when I've reached this goal?

Goal:

Target date:

Actions to complete this goal:

1.

2.

3.

4.

Why I'd love to achieve this goal:

How will I feel when I've reached this goal?

Goal:

Target date:

Actions to complete this goal:

1.

2.

3.

4.

Why I'd love to achieve this goal:

How will I feel when I've reached this goal?

Goal:

Target date:

Actions to complete this goal:

1.

2.

3.

4.

Why I'd love to achieve this goal:

How will I feel when I've reached this goal?

It's ok i
thing y
on tod
br

he only
ı focus
is your
th.

Soul Space

weekly planner

4 Major Goals I'm Focused On This Week:

| 1 | 2 | 3 | 4 |

Projects & Appointments For This Week	Target date	Actions & Yoga Practice For This Week	Target date
monday			
tuesday			
wednesday			
thursday			
friday			
saturday			
sunday			

date:

soul space

Today I am so **grateful** for...

My top 3 **inspired actions** for today are...

My **intentions** for today are...

I AM

I AM

I AM

What did I notice about my **yoga** practice today?

What did I **learn** today?

After today, what **behaviour** do I want to upgrade?

What **strengths** did I use today?

My Yoga Practice

Meditation	Inspiration
Yoga Practice	....

6.00

7.00

8.00

9.00

10.00

11.00

12.00

13.00

14.00

15.00

16.00

17.00

18.00

19.00

My Yoga Practice

heart space   date:

■ Meditation   ■ Inspiration

■ Yoga Practice   ■ ....

6.00

7.00

8.00

9.00

10.00

11.00

12.00

13.00

14.00

15.00

16.00

17.00

18.00

19.00

My Appreciation & gratitude list

Today, I am most inspired to do...

The mindset I wish to create today is...

I AM

I AM

I AM

What did I enjoy about today?

What challenged me today that I can learn from?

What new yoga pose would I like to perfect?

What did I do really well today?

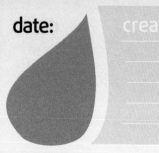

date:

creative space

The things I am **grateful** for in my life are...

	Meditation		Inspiration
	Yoga Practice		....

Today, I would **love** to do:

6.00
7.00

Today **i am focusing** on being...

I AM

I AM

I AM

8.00
9.00

What did I notice about my **thoughts** today?

10.00
11.00
12.00

What could I have handled **differently** today?

13.00
14.00

How can I open to **new** possibilities?

15.00
16.00
17.00

What am I **proud** of that came about today?

18.00

19.00

gratitude is Wisdom...

Meditation   Inspiration

Yoga Practice   ....

6.00

7.00

8.00

9.00

10.00

11.00

12.00

13.00

14.00

15.00

16.00

17.00

18.00

19.00

Today, I feel inspired to do...

I create my day with my thoughts, therefore...

I AM

I AM

I AM

What did I love about my yoga practice today?

In what ways would I like to grow?

What would I like to let go of?

What was my underlying motivation today?

date:

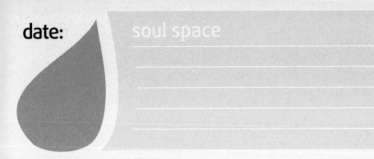

soul space

My Yoga Practice

When I am **grateful** I open up to more...

☐ Meditation   ☐ Inspiration

☐ Yoga Practice   ☐ ....

What would I do **today**, if it was my last?

6.00

7.00

Today...

8.00

I AM

I AM

9.00

I AM

10.00

What was **interesting** about today?

11.00

12.00

What am I not **seeing**?

13.00

14.00

What ideas would I like to **upgrade**?

15.00

16.00

17.00

When was I completely in the **moment** today?

18.00

19.00

heart space

date:

Today, I give **thanks** for...

Meditation　　Inspiration

Yoga Practice　　..................

6.00

7.00

8.00

9.00

10.00

11.00

12.00

13.00

14.00

15.00

16.00

17.00

18.00

19.00

My **inspired** actions for today are...

Today I **honour** how I feel and...

I AM

I AM

I AM

What was today's **lesson**?

How can I create a more **challenging** yoga practice?

What do I **know** that I'm not admitting?

What **strengths** did I use today?

weekly check - in

	09.00	13.00	17.00
	10.00	14.00	18.00
	11.00	15.00	19.00
	12.00	16.00	20.00

What have I achieved this week?

What's working with my practice and why is it working?

What's not working and what am I willing to do to upgrade it?

What is one thing I can do this week that will create the biggest results in my life?

What do I need to make a decision about?

How can I be more authentic?

What beliefs are holding me back and how can I upgrade them?

How can I open my chakras for more connection to my source?

Review Conscious Life Blueprint

Review Purpose Statement

Update 90-Day Planner

Add Actions to Weekly Planner

Plan Your Week

Old Habit >

New Habit >

New Actions >

New Affirmation/Mantra/Yoga Pose

weekly planner

4 Major Goals I'm Focused On This Week:

1	2	3	4

Projects & Appointments For This Week	Target date	Actions & Yoga Practice For This Week	Target date
monday			
tuesday			
wednesday			
thursday			
friday			
saturday			
sunday			

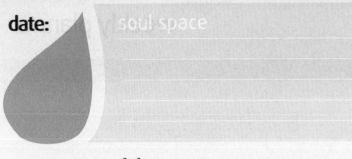

date:

soul space

My Yoga Practice

| Meditation | Inspiration |
| Yoga Practice | .... |

6.00

7.00

8.00

9.00

10.00

11.00

12.00

13.00

14.00

15.00

16.00

17.00

18.00

19.00

When I am grateful I open up to more...

What would I do today, if it was my last?

Today...
I AM
I AM
I AM

What was interesting about today?

What am I not seeing?

What ideas would I like to upgrade?

When was I completely in the moment today?

heart space

date:

Today, I give **thanks** for...

Meditation   Inspiration

Yoga Practice   ....

My **inspired** actions for today are...

6.00

7.00

Today I **honour** how I feel and...

8.00

I AM

I AM

9.00

I AM

10.00

What was today's **lesson**?

11.00

12.00

I AM awakening to my potential

How can I create a more **challenging** yoga practice?

13.00

14.00

15.00

What do I **know** that I'm not admitting?

16.00

17.00

What **strengths** did I use today?

18.00

19.00

date:

soul space

My Yoga Practice

Today I am so **grateful** for...

	Meditation		Inspiration
	Yoga Practice		....

My top 3 **inspired actions** for today are...

My **intentions** for today are...

I AM

I AM

I AM

What did I notice about my **yoga** practice today?

What did I **learn** today?

After today, what **behaviour** do I want to upgrade?

What **strengths** did I use today?

6.00

7.00

8.00

9.00

10.00

11.00

12.00

13.00

14.00

15.00

16.00

17.00

18.00

19.00

heart space

date:

My Appreciation & gratitude list

Meditation   Inspiration

Yoga Practice   ....

Today, I am most inspired to do...

6.00

7.00

The mindset I wish to create today is...

8.00   I AM

              I AM
9.00
              I AM

10.00

What did I enjoy about today?

11.00

12.00

What challenged me today that I can learn from?

13.00

14.00

15.00   What new yoga pose would I like to perfect?

16.00

17.00   What did I do really well today?

18.00

19.00

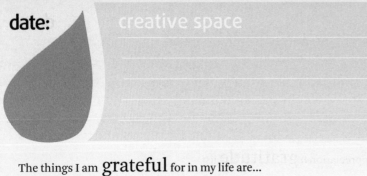

date:

creative space

My Yoga Practice

The things I am **grateful** for in my life are...

Today, I would **love** to do:

| Meditation | Inspiration |
| Yoga Practice | .... |

Today **i am focusing** on being...

I AM

I AM

I AM

What did I notice about my **thoughts** today?

What could I have handled **differently** today?

How can I open to **new** possibilities?

What am I **proud** of that came about today?

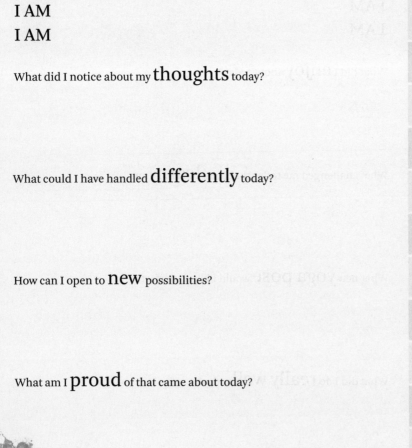

| 6.00 |
| 7.00 |
| 8.00 |
| 9.00 |
| 10.00 |
| 11.00 |
| 12.00 |
| 13.00 |
| 14.00 |
| 15.00 |
| 16.00 |
| 17.00 |
| 18.00 |
| 19.00 |

date:

gratitude is Wisdom...

Meditation   Inspiration

Yoga Practice   ....

6.00

7.00

Today, I feel inspired to do...

8.00

9.00

I create my day with my thoughts, therefore...

I AM

I AM

I AM

10.00

What did I love about my yoga practice today?

11.00

12.00

In what ways would I like to grow?

13.00

14.00

15.00

What would I like to let go of?

16.00

17.00

What was my underlying motivation today?

18.00

19.00

weekly check - in

	09.00	13.00	17.00
	10.00	14.00	18.00
	11.00	15.00	19.00
	12.00	16.00	20.00

What projects have I completed this week?

What's going well with my practice and why is it?

What do I find most challenging in my life right now?

What is one thing I can do this week that will create the biggest results in my life?

What am I happy about right now?

How can I be more empowered in my thoughts, words and actions?

What fears are holding me back and how can I overcome those?

How does my body feel? Am I feeling grounded?

Review Conscious Life Blueprint

Review Purpose Statement

Update 90-Day Planner

Add Actions to Weekly Planner

Plan Your Week

Old Habit >

New Habit >

New Actions >

New Affirmation/Mantra/Yoga Pose

weekly planner

4 Major Goals I'm Focused On This Week:

1   **2**   **3**   **4**

Projects & Appointments For This Week	Target date	Actions & Yoga Practice For This Week	Target date
monday			
tuesday			
wednesday			
thursday			
friday			
saturday			
sunday			

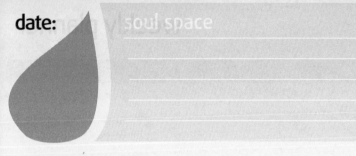

date:

soul space

My Yoga Practice

When I am **grateful** I open up to more...

What would I do **today**, if it was my last?

Today...
I AM
I AM
I AM

What was **interesting** about today?

What am I not **seeing**?

What ideas would I like to **upgrade**?

When was I completely in the **moment** today?

	Meditation		Inspiration
	Yoga Practice		....

6.00

7.00

8.00

9.00

10.00

11.00

12.00

13.00

14.00

15.00

16.00

17.00

18.00

19.00

date:

Today, I give **thanks** for...

Meditation   Inspiration

Yoga Practice   . . . .

My **inspired** actions for today are...

6.00

7.00

Today I **honour** how I feel and...

I AM

8.00

I AM

9.00

I AM

10.00

What was today's **lesson**?

11.00

12.00

How can I create a more **challenging** yoga practice?

13.00

14.00

15.00   What do I **know** that I'm not admitting?

16.00

17.00

What **strengths** did I use today?

18.00

19.00

date:

creative space

My Yoga Practice

What I **love** about my work is...

Meditation		Inspiration	
Yoga Practice		....	

Today I am inspired to take these **actions**:

6.00

7.00

I have a **beautiful** mind and...

I AM

I AM

8.00

I AM

9.00

What did I **learn** on the yoga mat today?

10.00

I AM happy, healthy & connected

11.00

12.00

How was my **mindset** today?

13.00

14.00

What new **habit** do I want to adopt into my life?

15.00

16.00

17.00

Where am I at this very moment?

18.00

19.00

dream space

date:

_____
_____
_____
_____
_____

I am so grateful for simple things like...

Meditation   Inspiration

Yoga Practice   ....

What is the best course of action to take today?

6.00

7.00

Today I am creative and...

8.00

I AM

I AM

9.00

I AM

10.00

Who AM I?

11.00

12.00

What am I supposed to do right now?

13.00

14.00

15.00

What new mindset do I want to adopt into my life?

16.00

17.00

How did my yoga practice feel today?

18.00

19.00

date:

soul space

My Yoga Practice

Today I am so **grateful** for...

| Meditation | | Inspiration |
| Yoga Practice | | .... |

My top 3 **inspired actions** for today are...

6.00	
7.00	

My **intentions** for today are...

I AM

I AM

I AM

| 8.00 | |
| 9.00 | |

What did I notice about my **yoga** practice today?

10.00	
11.00	
12.00	

What did I **learn** today?

| 13.00 | |
| 14.00 | |

After today, what **behaviour** do I want to upgrade?

15.00	
16.00	
17.00	

What **strengths** did I use today?

| 18.00 | |
| 19.00 | |

My Yoga Practice

Meditation Inspiration

Yoga Practice ....

6.00

7.00

8.00

9.00

10.00

11.00

12.00

13.00

14.00

15.00

16.00

17.00

18.00

19.00

heart space

date:

My Appreciation & gratitude list

Today, I am most inspired to do...

The mindset I wish to create today is...

I AM

I AM

I AM

What did I enjoy about today?

What challenged me today that I can learn from?

What new yoga pose would I like to perfect?

What did I do really well today?

weekly check - in

	09.00	13.00	17.00
	10.00	14.00	18.00
	11.00	15.00	19.00
	12.00	16.00	20.00

What have I achieved on my Conscious Life Blueprint this week?

What do I need to start or stop?

In my relationships, how can I communicate better?

What is one thing I can do this week that will create the biggest results in my life?

What am I proud about right now?

How can I be happier and more grateful?

What negative attitudes are holding me back and how can I overcome those?

How can I stretch myself further in my yoga practice?

Review Conscious Life Blueprint

Review Purpose Statement

Update 90-Day Planner

Add Actions to Weekly Planner

Plan Your Week

Old Habit >

New Habit >

New Actions >

New Affirmation/Mantra/Yoga Pose

weekly planner

Major Goals I'm Focused On This Week:			
1	**2**	**3**	**4**

Projects & Appointments For This Week	Target date	Actions & Yoga Practice For This Week	Target date
Monday			
Tuesday			
Wednesday			
Thursday			
Friday			
Saturday			
Sunday			

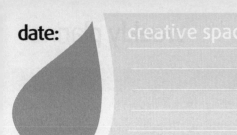

date:

creative space

The things I am grateful for in my life are...

Today, I would love to do:

Today i am focusing on being...

I AM

I AM

I AM

What did I notice about my thoughts today?

What could I have handled differently today?

How can I open to new possibilities?

What am I proud of that came about today?

Meditation   Inspiration

Yoga Practice   ....

6.00

7.00

8.00

9.00

10.00

11.00

12.00

13.00

14.00

15.00

16.00

17.00

18.00

19.00

dream space

date:

gratitude is Wisdom...

Meditation	Inspiration
Yoga Practice	....

6.00

7.00

Today, I feel inspired to do...

8.00

9.00

I create my day with my thoughts, therefore...

I AM

I AM

I AM

10.00

What did I love about my yoga practice today?

11.00

12.00

In what ways would I like to grow?

13.00

14.00

15.00

What would I like to let go of?

16.00

17.00

What was my underlying motivation today?

18.00

19.00

date:

soul space

My Yoga Practice

When I am grateful I open up to more...

What would I do today, if it was my last?

6.00

7.00

Today...

I AM

I AM

8.00

I AM

9.00

What was interesting about today?

10.00

11.00

12.00

What am I not seeing?

13.00

14.00

What ideas would I like to upgrade?

15.00

16.00

17.00

When was I completely in the moment today?

18.00

19.00

heart space

date:

■ Meditation   ■ Inspiration

■ Yoga Practice   ■ ....

6.00

7.00

8.00

9.00

10.00

11.00

12.00

13.00

14.00

15.00

16.00

17.00

18.00

19.00

Today, I give **thanks** for...

My **inspired** actions for today are...

Today I **honour** how I feel and...

I AM

I AM

I AM

What was today's **lesson**?

How can I create a more **challenging** yoga practice?

What do I **know** that I'm not admitting?

What **strengths** did I use today?

date:

soul space

My Yoga Practice

When I am **grateful** I open up to more...

- Meditation
- Yoga Practice
- Inspiration
- ....

What would I do **today**, if it was my last?

6.00	
7.00	
8.00	

Today...

I AM

I AM

I AM

I AM pure awareness

9.00
10.00

What was **interesting** about today?

11.00
12.00

What am I not **seeing**?

13.00
14.00

What ideas would I like to **upgrade**?

15.00
16.00
17.00

When was I completely in the **moment** today?

18.00
19.00

heart space

date:

Meditation   Inspiration

Yoga Practice   ....

6.00

7.00

8.00

9.00

10.00

11.00

12.00

13.00

14.00

15.00

16.00

17.00

18.00

19.00

Today, I give **thanks** for...

My **inspired** actions for today are...

Today I **honour** how I feel and...

I AM

I AM

I AM

What was today's **lesson**?

How can I create a more **challenging** yoga practice?

What do I **know** that I'm not admitting?

What **strengths** did I use today?

weekly check - in

	09.00	13.00	17.00
	10.00	14.00	18.00
	11.00	15.00	19.00
	12.00	16.00	20.00

What major goals have I achieved this month?

How can I be more congruent with my thoughts, words and actions?

What are the biggest distractions to my yoga practice and how can I remove them?

What is one thing I can do this week that will create the biggest results in my life?

What am I committed to in my life right now?

How can I shine my light more?

What disempowering thoughts are holding me back and how can I upgrade those?

What new pose or asana can I incorporate into my current yoga practice?

- ☐ Review Conscious Life Blueprint
- ☐ Review Purpose Statement
- ☐ Update 90-Day Planner
- ☐ Add Actions to Weekly Planner
- ☐ Plan Your Week

Old Habit >

New Habit >

New Actions >

New Affirmation/Mantra/Yoga Pose

weekly planner

4 Major Goals I'm Focused On This Week:

1   **2**   **3**   **4**

Projects & Appointments For This Week	Target date	Actions & Yoga Practice For This Week	Target date
monday			
tuesday			
wednesday			
thursday			
friday			
saturday			
sunday			

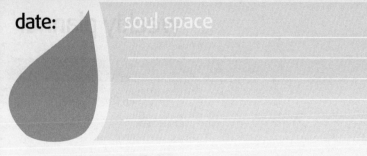

date:

soul space

Today I am so **grateful** for...

My top 3 **inspired actions** for today are...

My **intentions** for today are...

I AM

I AM

I AM

What did I notice about my **yoga** practice today?

What did I **learn** today?

After today, what **behaviour** do I want to upgrade?

What **strengths** did I use today?

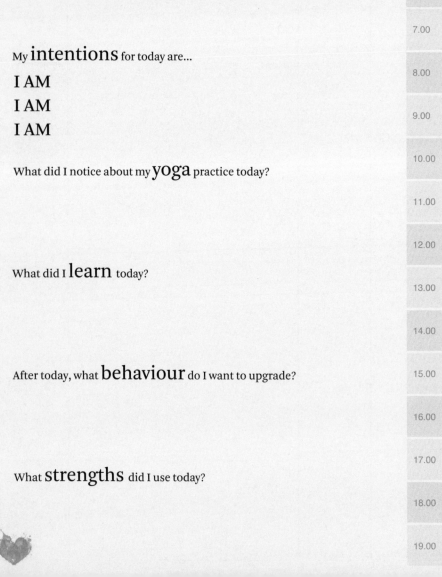

Meditation

Inspiration

Yoga Practice

....

6.00

7.00

8.00

9.00

10.00

11.00

12.00

13.00

14.00

15.00

16.00

17.00

18.00

19.00

My Yoga Practice

heart space

date:

My Appreciation & gratitude list

Meditation   Inspiration

Yoga Practice   . . . .

Today, I am most inspired to do...

6.00

7.00

The mindset I wish to create today is...

8.00

I AM

I AM

9.00

I AM

10.00

What did I enjoy about today?

11.00

12.00

What challenged me today that I can learn from?

13.00

14.00

What new yoga pose would I like to perfect?

15.00

16.00

17.00

What did I do really well today?

18.00

19.00

date:

creative space

My Yoga Practice

The things I am **grateful** for in my life are...

☐ Meditation   ☐ Inspiration

☐ Yoga Practice   ☐ ....

Today, I would **love** to do:

Today **i am focusing** on being...

I AM

I AM

I AM

What did I notice about my **thoughts** today?

What could I have handled **differently** today?

How can I open to **new** possibilities?

What am I **proud** of that came about today?

Time
6.00
7.00
8.00
9.00
10.00
11.00
12.00
13.00
14.00
15.00
16.00
17.00
18.00
19.00

dream space

date:

Meditation   Inspiration

Yoga Practice   ....

6.00

7.00

8.00

9.00

10.00

11.00

12.00

13.00

14.00

15.00

16.00

17.00

18.00

19.00

gratitude is Wisdom...

Today, I feel inspired to do...

I create my day with my thoughts, therefore...

I AM

I AM

I AM

What did I love about my yoga practice today?

I AM present

In what ways would I like to grow?

What would I like to let go of?

What was my underlying motivation today?

date:

My Yoga Practice

When I am **grateful** I open up to more...

☐ Meditation   ☐ Inspiration

☐ Yoga Practice   ☐ ....

What would I do **today**, if it was my last?

6.00

7.00

Today...

I AM

I AM

I AM

8.00

9.00

What was **interesting** about today?

10.00

11.00

12.00

What am I not **seeing**?

13.00

14.00

What ideas would I like to **upgrade**?

15.00

16.00

17.00

When was I completely in the **moment** today?

18.00

19.00

My Yoga Practice

Meditation   Inspiration

Yoga Practice   ....

6.00

7.00

8.00

9.00

10.00

11.00

12.00

13.00

14.00

15.00

16.00

17.00

18.00

19.00

heart space   **date:**

Today, I give **thanks** for...

My **inspired** actions for today are...

Today I **honour** how I feel and...

I AM

I AM

I AM

What was today's **lesson**?

How can I create a more **challenging** yoga practice?

What do I **know** that I'm not admitting?

What **strengths** did I use today?

weekly check - in

	09.00	13.00	17.00
	10.00	14.00	18.00
	11.00	15.00	19.00
	12.00	16.00	20.00

What have I achieved this week?

What's working with my practice and why is it working?

What's not working and what am I willing to do to upgrade it?

What is one thing I can do this week that will create the biggest results in my life?

What do I need to make a decision about?

How can I be more authentic?

What beliefs are holding me back and how can I upgrade them?

How can I open my chakras for more connection to my source?

- Review Conscious Life Blueprint
- Review Purpose Statement
- Update 90-Day Planner
- Add Actions to Weekly Planner
- Plan Your Week

Old Habit >

New Habit >

New Actions >

New Affirmation/Mantra/Yoga Pose

weekly planner

1	2	3	4

Projects & Appointments For This Week	Target date	Actions & Yoga Practice For This Week	Target date
monday			
tuesday			
wednesday			
thursday			
friday			
saturday			
sunday			

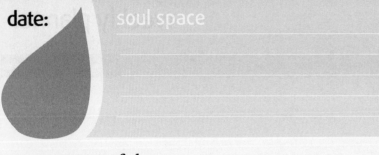

date: soul space

My Yoga Practice

When I am **grateful** I open up to more...

What would I do **today**, if it was my last?

6.00

7.00

Today...

I AM

I AM

I AM

8.00

9.00

10.00

What was **interesting** about today?

11.00

12.00

What am I not **seeing**?

13.00

14.00

What ideas would I like to **upgrade**?

15.00

16.00

17.00

When was I completely in the **moment** today?

18.00

19.00

My Yoga Practice

date:

Today, I give **thanks** for...

Meditation   Inspiration

Yoga Practice   ....

My **inspired** actions for today are...

6.00

7.00

Today I **honour** how I feel and...

8.00

I AM

I AM

9.00

I AM

10.00

What was today's **lesson**?

11.00

12.00

How can I create a more **challenging** yoga practice?

13.00

14.00

15.00

What do I **know** that I'm not admitting?

16.00

17.00

What **strengths** did I use today?

18.00

19.00

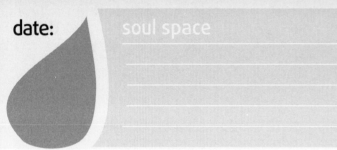

date:

soul space

My Yoga Practice

Today I am so **grateful** for...

My top 3 **inspired actions** for today are...

	Meditation		Inspiration
	Yoga Practice		....

My **intentions** for today are...

I AM

I AM

I AM

What did I notice about my **yoga** practice today?

What did I **learn** today?

After today, what **behaviour** do I want to upgrade?

What **strengths** did I use today?

| 6.00 |
| 7.00 |
| 8.00 |
| 9.00 |
| 10.00 |
| 11.00 |
| 12.00 |
| 13.00 |
| 14.00 |
| 15.00 |
| 16.00 |
| 17.00 |
| 18.00 |
| 19.00 |

heart space

date:

My Appreciation & gratitude list

Meditation

Inspiration

Yoga Practice

....

Today, I am most inspired to do...

6.00

7.00

The mindset I wish to create today is...

8.00

I AM

I AM

9.00

I AM

10.00

What did I enjoy about today?

11.00

12.00

What challenged me today that I can learn from?

13.00

14.00

What new yoga pose would I like to perfect?

15.00

16.00

17.00

What did I do really well today?

18.00

19.00

date:

creative space

The things I am **grateful** for in my life are...

Today, I would **love** to do:

Today **i am focusing** on being...

I AM

I AM

I AM

What did I notice about my **thoughts** today?

What could I have handled **differently** today?

How can I open to **new** possibilities?

What am I **proud** of that came about today?

My Yoga Practice

Meditation   Inspiration

Yoga Practice   ....

6.00

7.00

8.00

9.00

10.00

11.00

12.00

13.00

14.00

15.00

16.00

17.00

18.00

19.00

I AM happy, healthy & connected

gratitude is Wisdom...

Meditation   Inspiration

Yoga Practice   ·················

6.00

Today, I feel inspired to do...

7.00

8.00

I create my day with my thoughts, therefore...

I AM

I AM

9.00

I AM

10.00

What did I love about my yoga practice today?

11.00

12.00

In what ways would I like to grow?

13.00

14.00

15.00

What would I like to let go of?

16.00

17.00

What was my underlying motivation today?

18.00

19.00

weekly check - in

	09.00	13.00	17.00
	10.00	14.00	18.00
	11.00	15.00	19.00
	12.00	16.00	20.00

What projects have I completed this week?

What's going well with my practice and why is it?

What do I find most challenging in my life right now?

What is one thing I can do this week that will create the biggest results in my life?

What am I happy about right now?

How can I be more empowered in my thoughts, words and actions?

What fears are holding me back and how can I overcome those?

How does my body feel? Am I feeling grounded?

Review Conscious Life Blueprint

Review Purpose Statement

Update 90-Day Planner

Add Actions to Weekly Planner

Plan Your Week

Old Habit >

New Habit >

New Actions >

New Affirmation/Mantra/Yoga Pose

weekly planner

1	2	3	4

Projects & Appointments For This Week	Target date	Actions & Yoga Practice For This Week	Target date
monday			
tuesday			
wednesday			
thursday			
friday			
saturday			
sunday			

date: soul space

My Yoga Practice

When I am **grateful** I open up to more...

Meditation   Inspiration

Yoga Practice   ....

What would I do **today**, if it was my last?

6.00

| 7.00 |

Today...

I AM

I AM

I AM

| 8.00 |

| 9.00 |

What was **interesting** about today?

| 10.00 |

| 11.00 |

| 12.00 |

What am I not **seeing**?

| 13.00 |

| 14.00 |

What ideas would I like to **upgrade**?

| 15.00 |

| 16.00 |

| 17.00 |

When was I completely in the **moment** today?

| 18.00 |

| 19.00 |

date:

Meditation   Inspiration

Yoga Practice   ....

6.00

7.00

8.00

9.00

10.00

11.00

12.00

13.00

14.00

15.00

16.00

17.00

18.00

19.00

Today, I give **thanks** for...

My **inspired** actions for today are...

Today I **honour** how I feel and...

I AM

I AM

I AM

What was today's **lesson**?

How can I create a more **challenging** yoga practice?

What do I **know** that I'm not admitting?

What **strengths** did I use today?

date: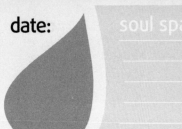

soul space

My Yoga Practice

When I am **grateful** I open up to more...

| | Meditation | | Inspiration |
| | Yoga Practice | | .... |

What would I do **today**, if it was my last?

I AM awakening to my potential

| 6.00 |
| 7.00 |

Today...

I AM

I AM

I AM

| 8.00 |
| 9.00 |

What was **interesting** about today?

| 10.00 |
| 11.00 |
| 12.00 |

What am I not **seeing**?

| 13.00 |
| 14.00 |

What ideas would I like to **upgrade**?

| 15.00 |
| 16.00 |
| 17.00 |

When was I completely in the **moment** today?

| 18.00 |

| 19.00 |

My Yoga Practice

date:

Today, I give **thanks** for...

Meditation   Inspiration

Yoga Practice   ....

My **inspired** actions for today are...

6.00

7.00

Today I **honour** how I feel and...

8.00   **I AM**

I AM

9.00   **I AM**

10.00   What was today's **lesson**?

11.00

12.00

How can I create a more **challenging** yoga practice?

13.00

14.00

15.00   What do I **know** that I'm not admitting?

16.00

17.00

What **strengths** did I use today?

18.00

19.00

date:

soul space

My Yoga Practice

Today I am so **grateful** for...

	Meditation		Inspiration
	Yoga Practice		....

My top 3 **inspired actions** for today are...

6.00

7.00

My **intentions** for today are...

I AM

I AM

I AM

8.00

9.00

What did I notice about my **yoga** practice today?

10.00

11.00

12.00

What did I **learn** today?

13.00

14.00

After today, what **behaviour** do I want to upgrade?

15.00

16.00

17.00

What **strengths** did I use today?

18.00

19.00

heart space

My Appreciation & gratitude list

Meditation   Inspiration

Yoga Practice   ....

Today, I am most inspired to do...

6.00

7.00

The mindset I wish to create today is...

8.00

I AM

I AM

9.00

I AM

10.00

What did I enjoy about today?

11.00

12.00

What challenged me today that I can learn from?

13.00

14.00

15.00

What new yoga pose would I like to perfect?

16.00

17.00

What did I do really well today?

18.00

19.00

weekly check - in

	09.00	13.00	17.00
	10.00	14.00	18.00
	11.00	15.00	19.00
	12.00	16.00	20.00

What have I achieved on my Conscious Life Blueprint this week?

What do I need to start or stop?

In my relationships, how can I communicate better?

What is one thing I can do this week that will create the biggest results in my life?

What am I proud about right now?

How can I be happier and more grateful?

What negative attitudes are holding me back and how can I overcome those?

How can I stretch myself further in my yoga practice?

Review Conscious Life Blueprint

Review Purpose Statement

Update 90-Day Planner

Add Actions to Weekly Planner

Plan Your Week

Old Habit >

New Habit >

New Actions >

New Affirmation/Mantra/Yoga Pose

weekly planner

4 Major Goals I'm Focused On This Week:

1	2	3	4

Projects & Appointments For This Week	Target date	Actions & Yoga Practice For This Week	Target date
monday			
tuesday			
wednesday			
thursday			
friday			
saturday			
sunday			

date:

creative space

The things I am **grateful** for in my life are...

Meditation   Inspiration

Yoga Practice   ....

Today, I would **love** to do:

6.00

7.00

Today **i am focusing** on being...

I AM

I AM

I AM

8.00

9.00

What did I notice about my **thoughts** today?

10.00

11.00

12.00

What could I have handled **differently** today?

13.00

14.00

How can I open to **new** possibilities?

15.00

16.00

17.00

What am I **proud** of that came about today?

18.00

19.00

date:

Meditation
Inspiration

Yoga Practice
....

6.00

7.00

8.00

9.00

10.00

11.00

12.00

13.00

14.00

15.00

16.00

17.00

18.00

19.00

gratitude is Wisdom...

Today, I feel **inspired** to do...

I create my day with my **thoughts**, therefore...

I AM

I AM

I AM

What did I **love** about my yoga practice today?

In what ways would I like to **grow**?

What would I like to **let go** of?

What was my underlying **motivation** today?

date:

soul space
_____
_____
_____
_____
_____

When I am **grateful** I open up to more...

What would I do **today**, if it was my last?

Today...
I AM
I AM
I AM

What was **interesting** about today?

What am I not **seeing**?

What ideas would I like to **upgrade**?

When was I completely in the **moment** today?

My Yoga Practice
_____
_____
_____
_____
_____

■ Meditation   ■ Inspiration

■ Yoga Practice ■ ....

| 6.00 |
| 7.00 |
| 8.00 |
| 9.00 |
| 10.00 |
| 11.00 |
| 12.00 |
| 13.00 |
| 14.00 |
| 15.00 |
| 16.00 |
| 17.00 |
| 18.00 |
| 19.00 |

My Yoga Practice

Meditation

Inspiration

Yoga Practice

....

6.00

7.00

8.00

9.00

10.00

11.00

12.00

13.00

14.00

15.00

16.00

17.00

18.00

19.00

heart space

date:

Today, I give **thanks** for...

My **inspired** actions for today are...

Today I **honour** how I feel and...

I AM

I AM

I AM

What was today's **lesson**?

How can I create a more **challenging** yoga practice?

What do I **know** that I'm not admitting?

What **strengths** did I use today?

date:

creative space

What I **love** about my work is...

Meditation   Inspiration

Yoga Practice   ....

Today I am inspired to take these **actions**:

6.00	
7.00	
8.00	
9.00	

I have a **beautiful** mind and...

I AM

I AM

I AM

What did I **learn** on the yoga mat today?

10.00
11.00
12.00

How was my **mindset** today?

13.00
14.00

What new **habit** do I want to adopt into my life?

15.00
16.00
17.00

Where am I at this very moment?

18.00
19.00

date:

I am so grateful for **simple** things like...

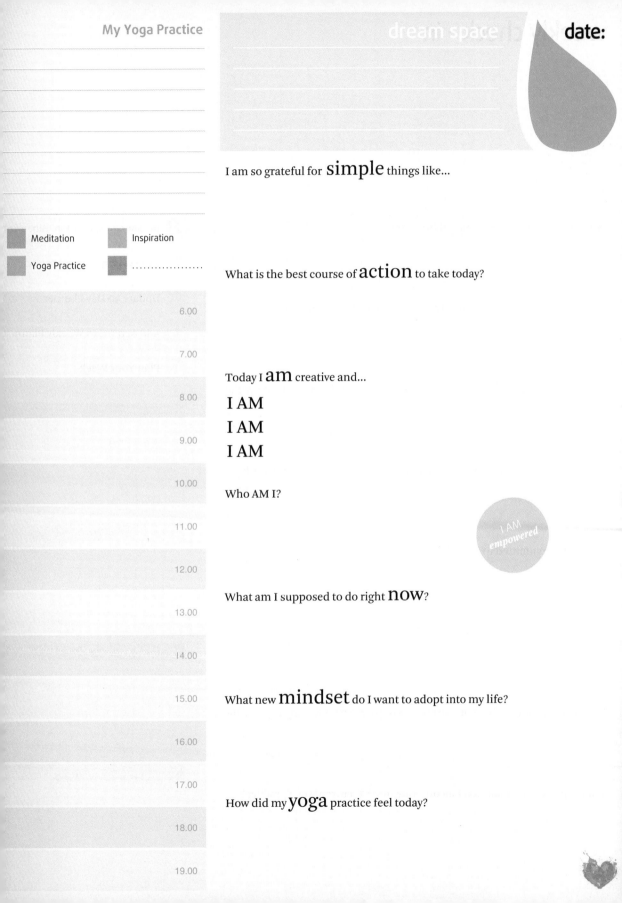

Meditation   Inspiration

Yoga Practice   ....

6.00

7.00

What is the best course of **action** to take today?

8.00

Today I **am** creative and...

9.00

I AM

I AM

I AM

10.00

Who AM I?

11.00

I AM empowered

12.00

13.00

What am I supposed to do right **now**?

14.00

15.00

What new **mindset** do I want to adopt into my life?

16.00

17.00

How did my **yoga** practice feel today?

18.00

19.00

weekly check - in

	09.00	13.00	17.00
	10.00	14.00	18.00
	11.00	15.00	19.00
	12.00	16.00	20.00

What major goals have I achieved this month?

How can I be more congruent with my thoughts, words and actions?

What are the biggest distractions to my yoga practice and how can I remove them?

What is one thing I can do this week that will create the biggest results in my life?

What am I committed to in my life right now?

How can I shine my light more?

What disempowering thoughts are holding me back and how can I upgrade those?

What new pose or asana can I incorporate into my current yoga practice?

Review Conscious Life Blueprint

Review Purpose Statement

Update 90-Day Planner

Add Actions to Weekly Planner

Plan Your Week

Old Habit >

New Habit >

New Actions >

New Affirmation/Mantra/Yoga Pose

weekly planner

4 Major Goals I'm Focused On This Week:			
1	**2**	**3**	**4**

Projects & Appointments For This Week	Target date	Actions & Yoga Practice For This Week	Target date
monday			
tuesday			
wednesday			
thursday			
friday			
saturday			
sunday			

date:

soul space

My Yoga Practice

Today I am so **grateful** for...

☐ Meditation   ☐ Inspiration

☐ Yoga Practice   ☐ ....

My top 3 **inspired actions** for today are...

6.00	
7.00	
8.00	
9.00	
10.00	
11.00	
12.00	
13.00	
14.00	
15.00	
16.00	
17.00	
18.00	
19.00	

My **intentions** for today are...

I AM

I AM

I AM

What did I notice about my **yoga** practice today?

What did I **learn** today?

After today, what **behaviour** do I want to upgrade?

What **strengths** did I use today?

date:

My Appreciation & gratitude list

Meditation	Inspiration
Yoga Practice	....

6.00

7.00

8.00

9.00

10.00

11.00

12.00

13.00

14.00

15.00

16.00

17.00

18.00

19.00

Today, I am most inspired to do...

The mindset I wish to create today is...

I AM

I AM

I AM

What did I enjoy about today?

What challenged me today that I can learn from?

What new yoga pose would I like to perfect?

What did I do really well today?

date:

creative space

My Yoga Practice

The things I am **grateful** for in my life are...

Today, I would **love** to do:

Today **i am focusing** on being...

I AM

I AM

I AM

What did I notice about my **thoughts** today?

What could I have handled **differently** today?

How can I open to **new** possibilities?

What am I **proud** of that came about today?

Meditation   Inspiration

Yoga Practice   ....

6.00

7.00

8.00

9.00

10.00

11.00

12.00

13.00

14.00

15.00

16.00

17.00

18.00

19.00

dream space

date:

gratitude is Wisdom...

Meditation   Inspiration

Yoga Practice   ·················

6.00

7.00

Today, I feel **inspired** to do...

8.00

9.00

I create my day with my **thoughts**, therefore...

I AM

I AM

I AM

10.00

What did I **love** about my yoga practice today?

11.00

12.00

13.00

In what ways would I like to **grow**?

14.00

15.00

What would I like to **let go** of?

16.00

17.00

What was my underlying **motivation** today?

18.00

19.00

date:

soul space

When I am grateful I open up to more...

What would I do today, if it was my last?

Today...
I AM
I AM
I AM

What was interesting about today?

What am I not seeing?

What ideas would I like to upgrade?

When was I completely in the moment today?

Meditation   Inspiration

Yoga Practice   ....

6.00

7.00

8.00

9.00

10.00

11.00

12.00

13.00

14.00

15.00

16.00

17.00

18.00

19.00

My Yoga Practice

heart space

date:

Today, I give **thanks** for...

Meditation   Inspiration

Yoga Practice   ....

6.00

7.00

8.00

9.00

10.00

11.00

12.00

13.00

14.00

15.00

16.00

17.00

18.00

19.00

My **inspired** actions for today are...

Today I **honour** how I feel and...

I AM

I AM

I AM

What was today's **lesson**?

How can I create a more **challenging** yoga practice?

What do I **know** that I'm not admitting?

What **strengths** did I use today?

weekly check - in

	09.00	13.00	17.00
	10.00	14.00	18.00
	11.00	15.00	19.00
	12.00	16.00	20.00

What have I achieved this week?

What's working with my practice and why is it working?

What's not working and what am I willing to do to upgrade it?

What is one thing I can do this week that will create the biggest results in my life?

What do I need to make a decision about?

How can I be more authentic?

What beliefs are holding me back and how can I upgrade them?

How can I open my chakras for more connection to my source?

Review Conscious Life Blueprint

Review Purpose Statement

Update 90-Day Planner

Add Actions to Weekly Planner

Plan Your Week

Old Habit >

New Habit >

New Actions >

New Affirmation/Mantra/Yoga Pose

weekly planner

1	2	3	4

Projects & Appointments For This Week	Target date	Actions & Yoga Practice For This Week	Target date
monday			
tuesday			
wednesday			
thursday			
friday			
saturday			
sunday			

date:

creative space

My Yoga Practice

What I **love** about my work is...

☐ Meditation   ☐ Inspiration

☐ Yoga Practice   ☐ ....

Today I am inspired to take these **actions**:

6.00

7.00

I have a **beautiful** mind and...

I AM

8.00

I AM

I AM

9.00

What did I **learn** on the yoga mat today?

10.00

11.00

12.00

How was my **mindset** today?

13.00

14.00

What new **habit** do I want to adopt into my life?

15.00

16.00

17.00

Where am I at this very moment?

18.00

19.00

dream space

date:

I am so grateful for **simple** things like...

Meditation   Inspiration

Yoga Practice   ....

What is the best course of **action** to take today?

6.00

7.00

Today I **am** creative and...

8.00

I AM

I AM

9.00

I AM

10.00

Who AM I?

11.00

12.00

What am I supposed to do right **now**?

13.00

14.00

15.00

What new **mindset** do I want to adopt into my life?

16.00

17.00

How did my **yoga** practice feel today?

18.00

19.00

date:

soul space
_____
_____
_____
_____

Today I am so **grateful** for...

My top 3 **inspired actions** for today are...

My **intentions** for today are...

I AM

I AM

I AM

What did I notice about my **yoga** practice today?

What did I **learn** today?

After today, what **behaviour** do I want to upgrade?

What **strengths** did I use today?

My Yoga Practice
_____
_____
_____
_____
_____
_____
_____

☐ Meditation   ☐ Inspiration

☐ Yoga Practice   ☐ ....

6.00	
7.00	
8.00	
9.00	
10.00	
11.00	
12.00	
13.00	
14.00	
15.00	
16.00	
17.00	
18.00	
19.00	

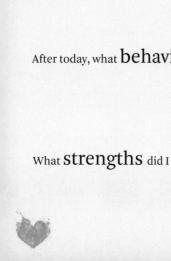

heart space

date:

My Appreciation & gratitude list

Meditation   Inspiration

Yoga Practice   ....

6.00

7.00

Today, I am most inspired to do...

8.00

The mindset I wish to create today is...

I AM

I AM

9.00

I AM

10.00

What did I enjoy about today?

11.00

12.00

What challenged me today that I can learn from?

13.00

14.00

15.00

What new yoga pose would I like to perfect?

I AM
happy,
healthy &
connected

16.00

17.00

What did I do really well today?

18.00

19.00

date:

creative space

My Yoga Practice

The things I am **grateful** for in my life are...

Today, I would **love** to do:

Today **i am focusing** on being...

I AM

I AM

I AM

What did I notice about my **thoughts** today?

What could I have handled **differently** today?

How can I open to **new** possibilities?

What am I **proud** of that came about today?

	Meditation		Inspiration
	Yoga Practice		....

6.00

7.00

8.00

9.00

10.00

11.00

12.00

13.00

14.00

15.00

16.00

17.00

18.00

19.00

gratitude is Wisdom...

Meditation   Inspiration

Yoga Practice   ....

Today, I feel inspired to do...

6.00

7.00

I create my day with my thoughts, therefore...

8.00

I AM

I AM

9.00

I AM

10.00

What did I love about my yoga practice today?

11.00

I AM
pure
awareness

12.00

In what ways would I like to grow?

13.00

14.00

15.00

What would I like to let go of?

16.00

17.00

What was my underlying motivation today?

18.00

19.00

weekly check - in

09.00	13.00	17.00
10.00	14.00	18.00
11.00	15.00	19.00
12.00	16.00	20.00

What projects have I completed this week?

What's going well with my practice and why is it?

What do I find most challenging in my life right now?

What is one thing I can do this week that will create the biggest results in my life?

What am I happy about right now?

How can I be more empowered in my thoughts, words and actions?

What fears are holding me back and how can I overcome those?

How does my body feel? Am I feeling grounded?

Review Conscious Life Blueprint

Review Purpose Statement

Update 90-Day Planner

Add Actions to Weekly Planner

Plan Your Week

Old Habit >

New Habit >

New Actions >

New Affirmation/Mantra/Yoga Pose

weekly planner

1　　　**2**　　　**3**　　　**4**

Projects & Appointments For This Week	Target date	Actions & Yoga Practice For This Week	Target date
monday			
tuesday			
wednesday			
thursday			
friday			
saturday			
sunday			

date:

soul space

When I am **grateful** I open up to more...

What would I do **today**, if it was my last?

Today...
I AM
I AM
I AM

What was **interesting** about today?

What am I not **seeing**?

What ideas would I like to **upgrade**?

When was I completely in the **moment** today?

My Yoga Practice

	Meditation		Inspiration
	Yoga Practice		....

6.00

7.00

8.00

9.00

10.00

11.00

12.00

13.00

14.00

15.00

16.00

17.00

18.00

19.00

heart space

date:

Meditation   Inspiration

Yoga Practice   ....

6.00

7.00

8.00

9.00

10.00

11.00

12.00

13.00

14.00

15.00

16.00

17.00

18.00

19.00

Today, I give **thanks** for...

My **inspired** actions for today are...

Today I **honour** how I feel and...

I AM

I AM

I AM

What was today's **lesson**?

How can I create a more **challenging** yoga practice?

What do I **know** that I'm not admitting?

What **strengths** did I use today?

date:

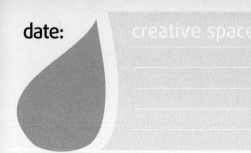

creative space

What I **love** about my work is...

Meditation   Inspiration

Yoga Practice   ....

Today I am inspired to take these **actions**:

6.00

7.00

I have a **beautiful** mind and...

8.00

I AM

I AM

9.00

I AM

What did I **learn** on the yoga mat today?

10.00

11.00

12.00

How was my **mindset** today?

13.00

14.00

What new **habit** do I want to adopt into my life?

15.00

16.00

17.00

Where am I at this very moment?

18.00

19.00

dream space

date:

I am so grateful for simple things like...

Meditation   Inspiration

Yoga Practice   . . . .

What is the best course of action to take today?

6.00

7.00

Today I am creative and...

8.00

I AM

I AM

9.00

I AM

10.00

Who AM I?

11.00

12.00

What am I supposed to do right now?

13.00

14.00

15.00   What new mindset do I want to adopt into my life?

16.00

17.00

How did my yoga practice feel today?

18.00

19.00

date:

soul space

Today I am so **grateful** for...

Meditation   Inspiration

Yoga Practice   ....

My top 3 **inspired actions** for today are...

My **intentions** for today are...

I AM

I AM

I AM

What did I notice about my **yoga** practice today?

What did I **learn** today?

After today, what **behaviour** do I want to upgrade?

What **strengths** did I use today?

6.00

7.00

8.00

9.00

10.00

11.00

12.00

13.00

14.00

15.00

16.00

17.00

18.00

19.00

My Yoga Practice

Meditation   Inspiration

Yoga Practice   ·················

	6.00
	7.00
	8.00
	9.00
	10.00
	11.00
	12.00
	13.00
	14.00
	15.00
	16.00
	17.00
	18.00
	19.00

date:

My Appreciation & gratitude list

Today, I am most inspired to do...

The mindset I wish to create today is...

I AM

I AM

I AM

I AM peaceful

What did I enjoy about today?

What challenged me today that I can learn from?

What new yoga pose would I like to perfect?

What did I do really well today?

weekly check - in

	09.00	13.00	17.00
	10.00	14.00	18.00
	11.00	15.00	19.00
	12.00	16.00	20.00

What have I achieved on my Conscious Life Blueprint this week?

What do I need to start or stop?

In my relationships, how can I communicate better?

What is one thing I can do this week that will create the biggest results in my life?

What am I proud about right now?

How can I be happier and more grateful?

What negative attitudes are holding me back and how can I overcome those?

How can I stretch myself further in my yoga practice?

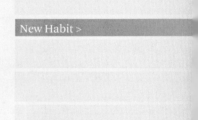

Review Conscious Life Blueprint

Review Purpose Statement

Update 90-Day Planner

Add Actions to Weekly Planner

Plan Your Week

Old Habit >

New Habit >

New Actions >

New Affirmation/Mantra/Yoga Pose

weekly planner

4 Major Goals I'm Focused On This Week:			
1	**2**	**3**	**4**

Projects & Appointments For This Week	Target date	Actions & Yoga Practice For This Week	Target date
monday			
tuesday			
wednesday			
thursday			
friday			
saturday			
sunday			

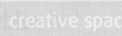
date:

creative space

The things I am **grateful** for in my life are...

Meditation ☐ Inspiration

Yoga Practice ☐ ....

Today, I would **love** to do:

6.00

7.00

Today **i am focusing** on being...

I AM

I AM

8.00

I AM

9.00

What did I notice about my **thoughts** today?

10.00

11.00

12.00

What could I have handled **differently** today?

13.00

14.00

How can I open to **new** possibilities?

15.00

16.00

17.00

What am I **proud** of that came about today?

18.00

19.00

dream space

date:

_____
_____
_____
_____
_____
_____
_____
_____
_____
_____
_____

gratitude is Wisdom...

Meditation   Inspiration

Yoga Practice   ....

Today, I feel **inspired** to do...

6.00

7.00

I create my day with my **thoughts**, therefore...

8.00   I AM

         I AM
9.00
         I AM

10.00   What did I **love** about my yoga practice today?

11.00

12.00

In what ways would I like to **grow**?

13.00

14.00

15.00   What would I like to **let go** of?

16.00

17.00   What was my underlying **motivation** today?

18.00

19.00

date:

soul space

My Yoga Practice

When I am **grateful** I open up to more...

What would I do **today**, if it was my last?

Today...
I AM
I AM
I AM

What was **interesting** about today?

What am I not **seeing**?

What ideas would I like to **upgrade**?

When was I completely in the **moment** today?

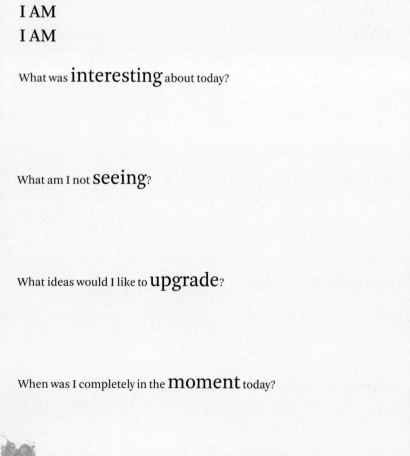

Meditation   Inspiration

Yoga Practice   ....

6.00

7.00

8.00

9.00

10.00

11.00

12.00

13.00

14.00

15.00

16.00

17.00

18.00

19.00

date:

- Meditation
- Inspiration
- Yoga Practice
- ....

6.00

7.00

8.00

9.00

10.00

11.00

12.00

13.00

14.00

15.00

16.00

17.00

18.00

19.00

Today, I give **thanks** for...

My **inspired** actions for today are...

Today I **honour** how I feel and...

I AM

I AM

I AM

What was today's **lesson**?

How can I create a more **challenging** yoga practice?

What do I **know** that I'm not admitting?

What **strengths** did I use today?

I AM present

date:

creative space

What I **love** about my work is...

Meditation   Inspiration

Yoga Practice   ....

Today I am inspired to take these **actions**:

6.00

7.00

I have a **beautiful** mind and...

I AM

I AM

I AM

8.00

9.00

What did I **learn** on the yoga mat today?

10.00

11.00

12.00

How was my **mindset** today?

13.00

14.00

What new **habit** do I want to adopt into my life?

15.00

16.00

17.00

Where am I at this very moment?

18.00

19.00

My Yoga Practice

Meditation   Inspiration

Yoga Practice   ....

6.00

7.00

8.00

9.00

10.00

11.00

12.00

13.00

14.00

15.00

16.00

17.00

18.00

19.00

dream space

date:

I am so grateful for **simple** things like...

What is the best course of **action** to take today?

Today I **am** creative and...

I AM

I AM

I AM

Who AM I?

What am I supposed to do right **now**?

What new **mindset** do I want to adopt into my life?

How did my **yoga** practice feel today?

weekly check - in

	09.00	13.00	17.00
	10.00	14.00	18.00
	11.00	15.00	19.00
	12.00	16.00	20.00

What major goals have I achieved this month?

How can I be more congruent with my thoughts, words and actions?

What are the biggest distractions to my yoga practice and how can I remove them?

What is one thing I can do this week that will create the biggest results in my life?

What am I committed to in my life right now?

How can I shine my light more?

What disempowering thoughts are holding me back and how can I upgrade those?

What new pose or asana can I incorporate into my current yoga practice?

Review Conscious Life Blueprint

Review Purpose Statement

Update 90-Day Planner

Add Actions to Weekly Planner

Plan Your Week

Old Habit >

New Habit >

New Actions >

New Affirmation/Mantra/Yoga Pose

weekly planner

4 Major Goals I'm Focused On This Week:			
1	**2**	**3**	**4**

Projects & Appointments For This Week	Target date	Actions & Yoga Practice For This Week	Target date
monday			
tuesday			
wednesday			
thursday			
friday			
saturday			
sunday			

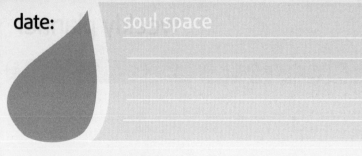

date:

soul space

My Yoga Practice

Today I am so **grateful** for...

▢ Meditation		▢ Inspiration
▢ Yoga Practice		▢ ....

My top 3 **inspired actions** for today are...

6.00

7.00

My **intentions** for today are...

I AM

I AM

I AM

8.00

9.00

What did I notice about my **yoga** practice today?

10.00

11.00

12.00

What did I **learn** today?

13.00

14.00

After today, what **behaviour** do I want to upgrade?

15.00

16.00

17.00

What **strengths** did I use today?

18.00

19.00

heart space

date:

My Appreciation & gratitude list

Meditation	Inspiration
Yoga Practice	....

6.00

Today, I am most inspired to do...

7.00

8.00

The mindset I wish to create today is...

I AM

I AM

9.00

I AM

I AM
peaceful

10.00

What did I enjoy about today?

11.00

12.00

What challenged me today that I can learn from?

13.00

14.00

15.00

What new yoga pose would I like to perfect?

16.00

17.00

What did I do really well today?

18.00

19.00

date:

creative space

The things I am **grateful** for in my life are...

Today, I would **love** to do:

Today **i am focusing** on being...

I AM

I AM

I AM

What did I notice about my **thoughts** today?

What could I have handled **differently** today?

How can I open to **new** possibilities?

What am I **proud** of that came about today?

Meditation   Inspiration

Yoga Practice   ....

6.00

7.00

8.00

9.00

10.00

11.00

12.00

13.00

14.00

15.00

16.00

17.00

18.00

19.00

dream space

date:

gratitude is Wisdom...

Meditation	Inspiration
Yoga Practice	....

6.00

7.00

Today, I feel **inspired** to do...

8.00

I create my day with my **thoughts**, therefore...

I AM

I AM

9.00

I AM

10.00

What did I **love** about my yoga practice today?

11.00

12.00

In what ways would I like to **grow**?

13.00

14.00

15.00

What would I like to **let go** of?

16.00

17.00

What was my underlying **motivation** today?

18.00

19.00

date:

soul space

_____
_____
_____
_____
_____

My Yoga Practice
_____
_____
_____
_____
_____
_____

When I am grateful I open up to more...

| Meditation | Inspiration |
| Yoga Practice | .... |

What would I do today, if it was my last?

6.00

7.00

Today...

I AM

I AM

I AM

8.00

9.00

What was interesting about today?

10.00

11.00

12.00

What am I not seeing?

13.00

14.00

What ideas would I like to upgrade?

15.00

16.00

17.00

When was I completely in the moment today?

18.00

19.00

date:

Meditation   Inspiration

Yoga Practice   ....

6.00

7.00

8.00

9.00

10.00

11.00

12.00

13.00

14.00

15.00

16.00

17.00

18.00

19.00

Today, I give **thanks** for...

My **inspired** actions for today are...

Today I **honour** how I feel and...

I AM

I AM

I AM

What was today's **lesson**?

How can I create a more **challenging** yoga practice?

What do I **know** that I'm not admitting?

What **strengths** did I use today?

90 day check-in

Welcome to your 90-day check-in! It's time to celebrate your achievements, identify what needs attention and reset your focus for the next 90 days. Use the answers to the following questions to plan your next quarter and to stay inspired and motivated towards your goals.

What major goals have I achieved this past 90 days?
What am I happy about?

Does my vision still inspire me or do I need to create a new one?
How can I be more aligned with my Conscious Life Blueprint?

What new potentials have I witnessed unfolding
in my life in the last 90 days?

What new mindset do I wish to develop?
What is no longer acceptable to me?

Am I embracing change or resisting it?
How can I open up to more inner expansion?

Am I honouring myself with enough self-love,
self-respect, self-care? How can I love myself more?
What do I need to say yes or no to?

What goal or project am I focusing on for the next 90 days?

What would I love to consciously create over the next 90 days?

Review Conscious Life Blueprint   Review Your Yearly Planner   Plan Your Week

Review Purpose Statement   Complete Next 90 Day Planner   Celebrate Your Progress!

90 day planner

Month:

Goal:

Target date:

Actions to complete this goal:

1.

2.

3.

4.

Why I'd love to achieve this goal:

How will I feel when I've reached this goal?

Goal:

Target date:

Actions to complete this goal:

1.

2.

3.

4.

Why I'd love to achieve this goal:

How will I feel when I've reached this goal?

Month:

Goal:

Target date:

Actions to complete this goal:

1.

2.

3.

4.

Why I'd love to achieve this goal:

How will I feel when I've reached this goal?

Goal:

Target date:

Actions to complete this goal:

1.

2.

3.

4.

Why I'd love to achieve this goal:

How will I feel when I've reached this goal?

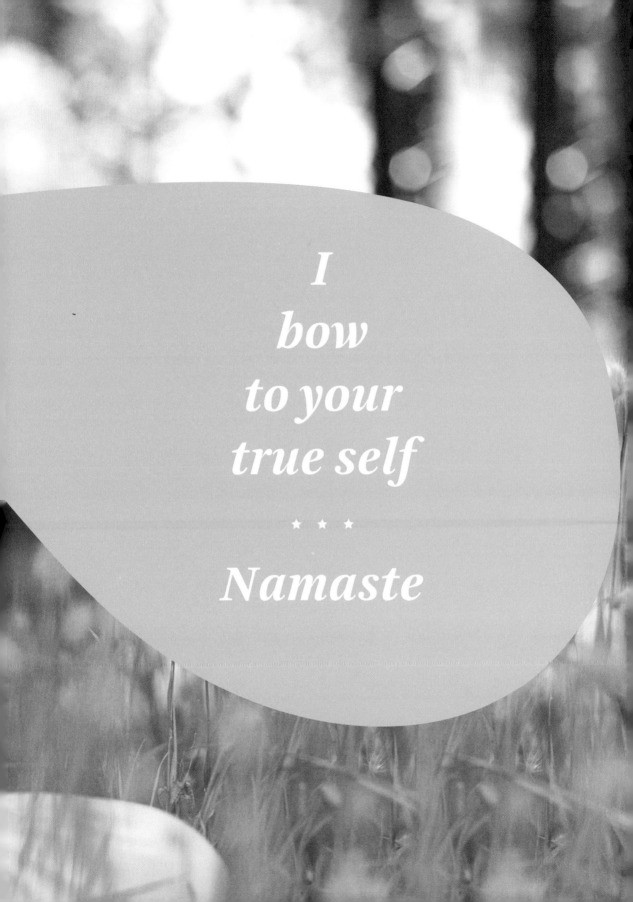

*I
bow
to your
true self*

* * *

Namaste

Soul Space

weekly planner

4 Major Goals I'm Focused On This Week:

1	2	3	4

Projects & Appointments For This Week	Target date	Actions & Yoga Practice For This Week	Target date
monday			
tuesday			
wednesday			
thursday			
friday			
saturday			
sunday			

date: my creative space

Today I am so **grateful** for...

My top 3 **inspired actions** for today are...

My **intentions** for today are...

I AM

I AM

I AM

What did I notice about my **yoga** practice today?

What did I **learn** today?

After today, what **behaviour** do I want to upgrade?

What **strengths** did I use today?

Meditation   Inspiration

Yoga Practice   ....

6.00

7.00

8.00

9.00

10.00

11.00

12.00

13.00

14.00

15.00

16.00

17.00

18.00

19.00

My Appreciation & gratitude list

Meditation   Inspiration

Yoga Practice   ....

Today, I am most inspired to do...

6.00

7.00

The mindset I wish to create today is...

8.00

I AM

I AM

9.00

I AM

10.00

What did I enjoy about today?

11.00

12.00

What challenged me today that I can learn from?

13.00

14.00

15.00

What new yoga pose would I like to perfect?

16.00

17.00

What did I do really well today?

18.00

19.00

date:

creative space

The things I am **grateful** for in my life are...

Today, I would **love** to do:

Today **i am focusing** on being...

I AM

I AM

I AM

What did I notice about my **thoughts** today?

What could I have handled **differently** today?

How can I open to **new** possibilities?

What am I **proud** of that came about today?

I AM happy, healthy & connected

☐ Meditation	☐ Inspiration
☐ Yoga Practice	☐ ....

6.00

7.00

8.00

9.00

10.00

11.00

12.00

13.00

14.00

15.00

16.00

17.00

18.00

19.00

dream space

date:

Meditation   Inspiration

Yoga Practice   ....

6.00

7.00

8.00

9.00

10.00

11.00

12.00

13.00

14.00

15.00

16.00

17.00

18.00

19.00

gratitude is Wisdom...

Today, I feel inspired to do...

I create my day with my thoughts, therefore...

I AM

I AM

I AM

What did I love about my yoga practice today?

In what ways would I like to grow?

What would I like to let go of?

What was my underlying motivation today?

date:

creative space

When I am **grateful** I open up to more...

Meditation   Inspiration

Yoga Practice   ....

What would I do **today**, if it was my last?

6.00

7.00

Today...
I AM
I AM
I AM

8.00

9.00

What was **interesting** about today?

10.00

11.00

12.00

What am I not **seeing**?

13.00

What ideas would I like to **upgrade**?

14.00

15.00

16.00

17.00

When was I completely in the **moment** today?

18.00

19.00

My Yoga Practice

dream space

date:

Today, I give **thanks** for...

■ Meditation   ■ Inspiration

■ Yoga Practice ■ ....

My **inspired** actions for today are...

6.00

7.00

Today I **honour** how I feel and...

I AM

I AM

I AM

8.00

9.00

10.00

What was today's **lesson**?

11.00

12.00

How can I create a more **challenging** yoga practice?

13.00

14.00

15.00

What do I **know** that I'm not admitting?

16.00

17.00

What **strengths** did I use today?

18.00

19.00

weekly check - in

	09.00	13.00	17.00
	10.00	14.00	18.00
	11.00	15.00	19.00
	12.00	16.00	20.00

What have I achieved this week?

What's working with my practice and why is it working?

What's not working and what am I willing to do to upgrade it?

What is one thing I can do this week that will create the biggest results in my life?

What do I need to make a decision about?

How can I be more authentic?

What beliefs are holding me back and how can I upgrade them?

How can I open my chakras for more connection to my source?

☐ Review Conscious Life Blueprint

☐ Review Purpose Statement

☐ Update 90-Day Planner

☐ Add Actions to Weekly Planner

☐ Plan Your Week

Old Habit >

New Habit >

New Actions >

New Affirmation/Mantra/Yoga Pose

weekly planner

1 **2** **3** **4**

Projects & Appointments For This Week	Target date	Actions & Yoga Practice For This Week	Target date
monday			
tuesday			
wednesday			
thursday			
friday			
saturday			
sunday			

date:

What I **love** about my work is...

Today I am inspired to take these **actions:**

I have a **beautiful** mind and...

I AM

I AM

I AM

What did I **learn** on the yoga mat today?

How was my **mindset** today?

What new **habit** do I want to adopt into my life?

Where am I at this very moment?

Meditation   Inspiration

Yoga Practice   ....

6.00

7.00

8.00

9.00

10.00

11.00

12.00

13.00

14.00

15.00

16.00

17.00

18.00

19.00

dream space

date:

I am so grateful for simple things like...

What is the best course of action to take today?

6.00

7.00

Today I am creative and...

8.00

I AM

I AM

9.00

I AM

10.00

Who AM I?

11.00

12.00

What am I supposed to do right now?

13.00

14.00

15.00

What new mindset do I want to adopt into my life?

16.00

17.00

How did my yoga practice feel today?

18.00

19.00

date:

creative space

Today I am so **grateful** for...

My top 3 **inspired actions** for today are...

My **intentions** for today are...

I AM

I AM

I AM

What did I notice about my **yoga** practice today?

What did I **learn** today?

After today, what **behaviour** do I want to upgrade?

What **strengths** did I use today?

Meditation   Inspiration

Yoga Practice   ....

6.00

7.00

8.00

9.00

10.00

11.00

12.00

13.00

14.00

15.00

16.00

17.00

18.00

19.00

My Yoga Practice

dream space

date:

My Appreciation & gratitude list

Meditation

Inspiration

Yoga Practice ....

Today, I am most inspired to do...

6.00

7.00

The mindset I wish to create today is...

I AM

I AM

8.00

9.00

I AM

10.00

What did I enjoy about today?

11.00

12.00

What challenged me today that I can learn from?

13.00

14.00

15.00

What new yoga pose would I like to perfect?

16.00

17.00

What did I do really well today?

18.00

19.00

date:

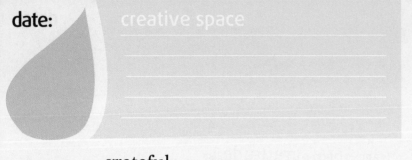

creative space

The things I am **grateful** for in my life are...

Today, I would **love** to do:

Today **i am focusing** on being...

I AM

I AM

I AM

What did I notice about my **thoughts** today?

What could I have handled **differently** today?

How can I open to **new** possibilities?

What am I **proud** of that came about today?

☐ Meditation   ☐ Inspiration

☐ Yoga Practice   ☐ ....

6.00

7.00

8.00

9.00

10.00

11.00

12.00

13.00

14.00

15.00

16.00

17.00

18.00

19.00

dream space

date:

gratitude is Wisdom...

Meditation   Inspiration

Yoga Practice   ....

I AM awakening to my potential

Today, I feel **inspired** to do...

6.00

7.00

I create my day with my **thoughts**, therefore...

I AM

I AM

I AM

8.00

9.00

10.00

What did I **love** about my yoga practice today?

11.00

12.00

In what ways would I like to **grow**?

13.00

14.00

15.00

What would I like to **let go** of?

16.00

17.00

What was my underlying **motivation** today?

18.00

19.00

weekly check - in

	09.00	13.00	17.00
	10.00	14.00	18.00
	11.00	15.00	19.00
	12.00	16.00	20.00

What projects have I completed this week?

What's going well with my practice and why is it?

What do I find most challenging in my life right now?

What is one thing I can do this week that will create the biggest results in my life?

What am I happy about right now?

How can I be more empowered in my thoughts, words and actions?

What fears are holding me back and how can I overcome those?

How does my body feel? Am I feeling grounded?

- Review Conscious Life Blueprint
- Review Purpose Statement
- Update 90-Day Planner
- Add Actions to Weekly Planner
- Plan Your Week

Old Habit >

New Habit >

New Actions >

New Affirmation/Mantra/Yoga Pose

weekly planner

1	2	3	4

Projects & Appointments For This Week	Target date	Actions & Yoga Practice For This Week	Target date
monday			
tuesday			
wednesday			
thursday			
friday			
saturday			
sunday			

date:

creative space

When I am grateful I open up to more...

■ Meditation   ■ Inspiration

■ Yoga Practice   ■ ....

What would I do today, if it was my last?

6.00

7.00

Today...
I AM
I AM
I AM

8.00

9.00

What was interesting about today?

10.00

11.00

What am I not seeing?

12.00

13.00

14.00

What ideas would I like to upgrade?

15.00

16.00

17.00

When was I completely in the moment today?

18.00

19.00

date:

Today, I give **thanks** for...

Meditation

Inspiration

Yoga Practice

....

My **inspired** actions for today are...

	6.00
	7.00

Today I **honour** how I feel and...

I AM

I AM

I AM

	8.00
	9.00

What was today's **lesson**?

	10.00
	11.00
	12.00

How can I create a more **challenging** yoga practice?

	13.00
	14.00

I AM present

What do I **know** that I'm not admitting?

	15.00
	16.00
	17.00

What **strengths** did I use today?

	18.00
	19.00

date:

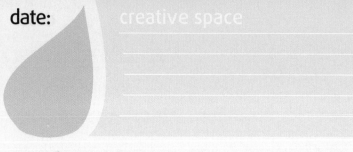

creative space

What I **love** about my work is...

Today I am inspired to take these **actions**:

I have a **beautiful** mind and...

I AM
I AM
I AM

What did I **learn** on the yoga mat today?

How was my **mindset** today?

What new **habit** do I want to adopt into my life?

Where am I at this very moment?

Meditation   Inspiration

Yoga Practice   ....

6.00

7.00

8.00

9.00

10.00

11.00

12.00

13.00

14.00

15.00

16.00

17.00

18.00

19.00

dream space

date:

Meditation   Inspiration

Yoga Practice   ....

6.00

7.00

8.00

9.00

10.00

11.00

12.00

13.00

14.00

15.00

16.00

17.00

18.00

19.00

I am so grateful for simple things like...

What is the best course of action to take today?

Today I am creative and...

I AM

I AM

I AM

Who AM I?

What am I supposed to do right now?

What new mindset do I want to adopt into my life?

How did my yoga practice feel today?

date:

Today I am so **grateful** for...

Meditation ☐ Inspiration ☐

Yoga Practice ☐ ....

My top 3 **inspired actions** for today are...

6.00

7.00

My **intentions** for today are...

I AM

I AM

I AM

I AM connected to my divine essence

8.00

9.00

What did I notice about my **yoga** practice today?

10.00

11.00

12.00

What did I **learn** today?

13.00

14.00

After today, what **behaviour** do I want to upgrade?

15.00

16.00

17.00

What **strengths** did I use today?

18.00

19.00

dream space

date:

My Appreciation & gratitude list

Meditation   Inspiration

Yoga Practice   ....

6.00

7.00

8.00

9.00

10.00

11.00

12.00

13.00

14.00

15.00

16.00

17.00

18.00

19.00

Today, I am most inspired to do...

The mindset I wish to create today is...

I AM

I AM

I AM

What did I enjoy about today?

What challenged me today that I can learn from?

What new yoga pose would I like to perfect?

What did I do really well today?

weekly check - in

	09.00	13.00	17.00
	10.00	14.00	18.00
	11.00	15.00	19.00
	12.00	16.00	20.00

What have I achieved on my Conscious Life Blueprint this week?

What do I need to start or stop?

In my relationships, how can I communicate better?

What is one thing I can do this week that will create the biggest results in my life?

What am I proud about right now?

How can I be happier and more grateful?

What negative attitudes are holding me back and how can I overcome those?

How can I stretch myself further in my yoga practice?

Review Conscious Life Blueprint

Review Purpose Statement

Update 90-Day Planner

Add Actions to Weekly Planner

Plan Your Week

Old Habit >

New Habit >

New Actions >

New Affirmation/Mantra/Yoga Pose

weekly planner

1	2	3	4

Projects & Appointments For This Week	Target date	Actions & Yoga Practice For This Week	Target date
monday			
tuesday			
wednesday			
thursday			
friday			
saturday			
sunday			

date:

creative space

The things I am **grateful** for in my life are...

Today, I would **love** to do:

Today **i am focusing** on being...

I AM

I AM

I AM

What did I notice about my **thoughts** today?

What could I have handled **differently** today?

How can I open to **new** possibilities?

What am I **proud** of that came about today?

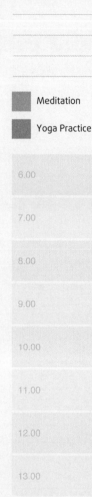

Meditation   Inspiration

Yoga Practice   ....

6.00

7.00

8.00

9.00

10.00

11.00

12.00

13.00

14.00

15.00

16.00

17.00

18.00

19.00

dream space

date:

gratitude is Wisdom...

Meditation   Inspiration

Yoga Practice   ....

6.00	
7.00	
8.00	
9.00	
10.00	
11.00	
12.00	
13.00	
14.00	
15.00	
16.00	
17.00	
18.00	
19.00	

Today, I feel inspired to do...

I create my day with my thoughts, therefore...

I AM

I AM

I AM

What did I love about my yoga practice today?

In what ways would I like to grow?

What would I like to let go of?

What was my underlying motivation today?

date:

creative space

When I am **grateful** I open up to more...

Meditation   Inspiration

Yoga Practice   ....

What would I do **today**, if it was my last?

6.00

7.00

Today...

I AM

I AM

I AM

8.00

9.00

What was **interesting** about today?

10.00

11.00

12.00

What am I not **seeing**?

13.00

14.00

What ideas would I like to **upgrade**?

15.00

16.00

17.00

When was I completely in the **moment** today?

18.00

19.00

My Yoga Practice

Meditation

Inspiration

Yoga Practice

....

6.00

7.00

8.00

9.00

10.00

11.00

12.00

13.00

14.00

15.00

16.00

17.00

18.00

19.00

dream space

date:

Today, I give **thanks** for...

My **inspired** actions for today are...

Today I **honour** how I feel and...

I AM

I AM

I AM

What was today's **lesson**?

How can I create a more **challenging** yoga practice?

What do I **know** that I'm not admitting?

What **strengths** did I use today?

date:

creative space

What I love about my work is...

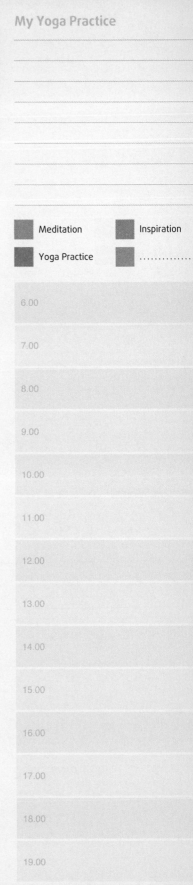

Meditation   Inspiration

Yoga Practice   ....

Today I am inspired to take these **actions:**

6.00

7.00

I have a beautiful mind and...

8.00

I AM

I AM

9.00

I AM

What did I learn on the yoga mat today?

10.00

11.00

12.00

How was my mindset today?

13.00

14.00

What new habit do I want to adopt into my life?

15.00

16.00

17.00

Where am I at this very moment?

18.00

19.00

dream space

date:

Meditation   Inspiration

Yoga Practice   ....

6.00

7.00

8.00

9.00

10.00

11.00

12.00

13.00

14.00

15.00

16.00

17.00

18.00

19.00

I am so grateful for simple things like...

What is the best course of action to take today?

Today I am creative and...

I AM

I AM

I AM

Who AM I?

What am I supposed to do right now?

What new mindset do I want to adopt into my life?

How did my yoga practice feel today?

I AM conscious

weekly check - in

	09.00	13.00	17.00
	10.00	14.00	18.00
	11.00	15.00	19.00
	12.00	16.00	20.00

What major goals have I achieved this month?

How can I be more congruent with my thoughts, words and actions?

What are the biggest distractions to my yoga practice and how can I remove them?

What is one thing I can do this week that will create the biggest results in my life?

What am I committed to in my life right now?

How can I shine my light more?

What disempowering thoughts are holding me back and how can I upgrade those?

What new pose or asana can I incorporate into my current yoga practice?

☐ Review Conscious Life Blueprint

☐ Review Purpose Statement

☐ Update 90-Day Planner

☐ Add Actions to Weekly Planner

☐ Plan Your Week

Old Habit >

New Habit >

New Actions >

New Affirmation/Mantra/Yoga Pose

weekly planner

1　　　　**2**　　　　**3**　　　　**4**

Projects & Appointments For This Week	Target date	Actions & Yoga Practice For This Week	Target date
monday			
tuesday			
wednesday			
thursday			
friday			
saturday			
sunday			

date:

Today I am so **grateful** for...

Meditation | Inspiration

Yoga Practice | ....

My top 3 **inspired actions** for today are...

6.00

7.00

My **intentions** for today are...

I AM

I AM

I AM

8.00

9.00

What did I notice about my **yoga** practice today?

10.00

11.00

12.00

What did I **learn** today?

13.00

14.00

After today, what **behaviour** do I want to upgrade?

15.00

16.00

17.00

What **strengths** did I use today?

18.00

19.00

My Yoga Practice

dream space

date:

Meditation	Inspiration
Yoga Practice	....

6.00

7.00

8.00

9.00

10.00

11.00

12.00

13.00

14.00

15.00

16.00

17.00

18.00

19.00

My Appreciation & gratitude list

Today, I am most inspired to do...

The mindset I wish to create today is...

I AM

I AM

I AM

What did I enjoy about today?

What challenged me today that I can learn from?

What new yoga pose would I like to perfect?

What did I do really well today?

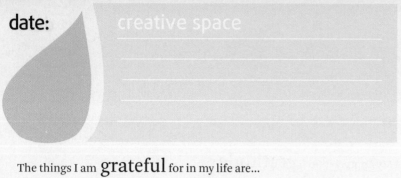

date:

creative space

The things I am **grateful** for in my life are...

Today, I would **love** to do:

Today **i am focusing** on being...

I AM

I AM

I AM

I AM
pure
awareness

What did I notice about my **thoughts** today?

What could I have handled **differently** today?

How can I open to **new** possibilities?

What am I **proud** of that came about today?

■ Meditation   ■ Inspiration

■ Yoga Practice   ■ ....

6.00

7.00

8.00

9.00

10.00

11.00

12.00

13.00

14.00

15.00

16.00

17.00

18.00

19.00

date:

gratitude is Wisdom...

Meditation   Inspiration

Yoga Practice   ....

Today, I feel **inspired** to do...

6.00	
7.00	
8.00	
9.00	
10.00	
11.00	
12.00	
13.00	
14.00	
15.00	
16.00	
17.00	
18.00	
19.00	

I create my day with my **thoughts**, therefore...

I AM

I AM

I AM

What did I **love** about my yoga practice today?

In what ways would I like to **grow**?

What would I like to **let go** of?

What was my underlying **motivation** today?

date:

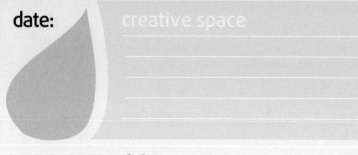

creative space

When I am **grateful** I open up to more...

| Meditation | Inspiration |
| Yoga Practice | .... |

What would I do **today**, if it was my last?

6.00

7.00

Today...
I AM
I AM
I AM

8.00

9.00

What was **interesting** about today?

10.00

11.00

12.00

What am I not **seeing**?

13.00

14.00

What ideas would I like to **upgrade**?

15.00

16.00

17.00

When was I completely in the **moment** today?

18.00

19.00

dream space

Meditation   Inspiration

Yoga Practice   . . . .

6.00

7.00

8.00

9.00

10.00

11.00

12.00

13.00

14.00

15.00

16.00

17.00

18.00

19.00

Today, I give **thanks** for...

My **inspired** actions for today are...

Today I **honour** how I feel and...

I AM

I AM

I AM

What was today's **lesson**?

How can I create a more **challenging** yoga practice?

What do I **know** that I'm not admitting?

What **strengths** did I use today?

weekly check - in

	09.00	13.00	17.00
	10.00	14.00	18.00
	11.00	15.00	19.00
	12.00	16.00	20.00

What have I achieved this week?

What's working with my practice and why is it working?

What's not working and what am I willing to do to upgrade it?

What is one thing I can do this week that will create the biggest results in my life?

What do I need to make a decision about?

How can I be more authentic?

What beliefs are holding me back and how can I upgrade them?

How can I open my chakras for more connection to my source?

Review Conscious Life Blueprint

Review Purpose Statement

Update 90-Day Planner

Add Actions to Weekly Planner

Plan Your Week

Old Habit >

New Habit >

New Actions >

New Affirmation/Mantra/Yoga Pose

weekly planner

4 Major Goals I'm Focused On This Week:

1	2	3	4

Projects & Appointments For This Week	Target date	Actions & Yoga Practice For This Week	Target date
monday			
tuesday			
wednesday			
thursday			
friday			
saturday			
sunday			

date:

creative space

What I love about my work is...

Meditation   Inspiration

Yoga Practice   ....

Today I am inspired to take these actions:

6.00

7.00

I have a beautiful mind and...

I AM

I AM   8.00

I AM

9.00

What did I learn on the yoga mat today?

10.00

11.00

12.00

How was my mindset today?

13.00

14.00

What new habit do I want to adopt into my life?

15.00

16.00

17.00

Where am I at this very moment?

18.00

19.00

date:

I am so grateful for **simple** things like...

Meditation   Inspiration

Yoga Practice   ·················

What is the best course of **action** to take today?

6.00

7.00

Today I **am** creative and...

8.00

I AM

I AM

9.00

I AM

10.00

Who AM I?

11.00

12.00

What am I supposed to do right **now**?

13.00

14.00

What new **mindset** do I want to adopt into my life?

15.00

16.00

17.00

How did my **yoga** practice feel today?

18.00

19.00

date:

creative space

My Yoga Practice

Today I am so **grateful** for...

Meditation   Inspiration

Yoga Practice   ....

My top 3 **inspired actions** for today are...

6.00

7.00

My **intentions** for today are...

I AM

I AM

I AM

8.00

9.00

What did I notice about my **yoga** practice today?

10.00

11.00

12.00

What did I **learn** today?

13.00

After today, what **behaviour** do I want to upgrade?

14.00

15.00

16.00

17.00

What **strengths** did I use today?

18.00

19.00

My Yoga Practice

- Meditation
- Inspiration
- Yoga Practice
- ....

	6.00
	7.00
	8.00
	9.00
	10.00
	11.00
	12.00
	13.00
	14.00
	15.00
	16.00
	17.00
	18.00
	19.00

dream space

date:

My Appreciation & gratitude list

Today, I am most inspired to do...

The mindset I wish to create today is...

I AM

I AM

I AM

What did I enjoy about today?

What challenged me today that I can learn from?

What new yoga pose would I like to perfect?

I AM happy, healthy & connected

What did I do really well today?

date:

creative space

The things I am grateful for in my life are...

Meditation   Inspiration

Yoga Practice   ....

Today, I would love to do:

6.00

7.00

Today i am focusing on being...

8.00

I AM

I AM

9.00

I AM

10.00

What did I notice about my thoughts today?

11.00

12.00

What could I have handled differently today?

13.00

14.00

How can I open to new possibilities?

15.00

16.00

17.00

What am I proud of that came about today?

18.00

19.00

dream space

date:

Meditation   Inspiration

Yoga Practice   · · · · · · · · · · · · · ·

6.00

7.00

8.00

9.00

10.00

11.00

12.00

13.00

14.00

15.00

16.00

17.00

18.00

19.00

gratitude is Wisdom...

Today, I feel **inspired** to do...

I create my day with my **thoughts**, therefore...

I AM

I AM

I AM

What did I **love** about my yoga practice today?

In what ways would I like to **grow**?

What would I like to **let go** of?

What was my underlying **motivation** today?

weekly check - in

	09.00	13.00	17.00
	10.00	14.00	18.00
	11.00	15.00	19.00
	12.00	16.00	20.00

What projects have I completed this week?

What's going well with my practice and why is it?

What do I find most challenging in my life right now?

What is one thing I can do this week that will create the biggest results in my life?

What am I happy about right now?

How can I be more empowered in my thoughts, words and actions?

What fears are holding me back and how can I overcome those?

How does my body feel? Am I feeling grounded?

 Review Conscious Life Blueprint

 Review Purpose Statement

 Update 90-Day Planner

 Add Actions to Weekly Planner

 Plan Your Week

Old Habit >

New Habit >

New Actions >

New Affirmation/Mantra/Yoga Pose

weekly planner

| 1 | 2 | 3 | 4 |

Projects & Appointments For This Week	Target date	Actions & Yoga Practice For This Week	Target date
monday			
tuesday			
wednesday			
thursday			
friday			
saturday			
sunday			

date:

When I am grateful I open up to more...

What would I do today, if it was my last?

Today...
I AM
I AM
I AM

What was interesting about today?

What am I not seeing?

What ideas would I like to upgrade?

When was I completely in the moment today?

My Yoga Practice

▢ Meditation   ▢ Inspiration

▢ Yoga Practice ▢ ....

6.00

7.00

8.00

9.00

10.00

11.00

12.00

13.00

14.00

15.00

16.00

17.00

18.00

19.00

date:

Meditation   Inspiration

Yoga Practice   ....

6.00

7.00

8.00

9.00

10.00

11.00

12.00

13.00

14.00

15.00

16.00

17.00

18.00

19.00

Today, I give **thanks** for...

My **inspired** actions for today are...

Today I **honour** how I feel and...

I AM

I AM

I AM

What was today's **lesson**?

How can I create a more **challenging** yoga practice?

What do I **know** that I'm not admitting?

What **strengths** did I use today?

date:

creative space

What I love about my work is...

Today I am inspired to take these actions:

I have a beautiful mind and...

I AM

I AM

I AM

What did I learn on the yoga mat today?

How was my mindset today?

What new habit do I want to adopt into my life?

Where am I at this very moment?

My Yoga Practice

Meditation   Inspiration

Yoga Practice   ....

6.00

7.00

8.00

9.00

10.00

11.00

12.00

13.00

14.00

15.00

16.00

17.00

18.00

19.00

My Yoga Practice

date:

I am so grateful for **simple** things like...

- Meditation
- Inspiration
- Yoga Practice
- ....

6.00	
7.00	
8.00	
9.00	
10.00	
11.00	
12.00	
13.00	
14.00	
15.00	
16.00	
17.00	
18.00	
19.00	

What is the best course of **action** to take today?

Today I **am** creative and...

I AM

I AM

I AM

Who AM I?

What am I supposed to do right **now**?

What new **mindset** do I want to adopt into my life?

How did my **yoga** practice feel today?

date:

My Yoga Practice

Today I am so grateful for...

Meditation   Inspiration

Yoga Practice   ....

My top 3 inspired actions for today are...

6.00

7.00

My intentions for today are...

I AM

I AM   8.00

I AM

9.00

What did I notice about my yoga practice today?

10.00

11.00

12.00

What did I learn today?

13.00

14.00

After today, what behaviour do I want to upgrade?   15.00

16.00

17.00

What strengths did I use today?

18.00

19.00

dream space

date:

My Appreciation & gratitude list

Meditation   Inspiration

Yoga Practice   ....

6.00

7.00

8.00

9.00

10.00

11.00

12.00

13.00

14.00

15.00

16.00

17.00

18.00

19.00

Today, I am most inspired to do...

The mindset I wish to create today is...

I AM

I AM

I AM

What did I enjoy about today?

What challenged me today that I can learn from?

What new yoga pose would I like to perfect?

What did I do really well today?

weekly check - in

	09.00	13.00	17.00
	10.00	14.00	18.00
	11.00	15.00	19.00
	12.00	16.00	20.00

What have I achieved on my Conscious Life Blueprint this week?

What do I need to start or stop?

In my relationships, how can I communicate better?

What is one thing I can do this week that will create the biggest results in my life?

What am I proud about right now?

How can I be happier and more grateful?

What negative attitudes are holding me back and how can I overcome those?

How can I stretch myself further in my yoga practice?

Review Conscious Life Blueprint

Review Purpose Statement

Update 90-Day Planner

Add Actions to Weekly Planner

Plan Your Week

Old Habit >

New Habit >

New Actions >

New Affirmation/Mantra/Yoga Pose

weekly planner

4 Major Goals I'm Focused On This Week:

1	2	3	4

Projects & Appointments For This Week	Target date	Actions & Yoga Practice For This Week	Target date
monday			
tuesday			
wednesday			
thursday			
friday			
saturday			
sunday			

date:

creative space

The things I am **grateful** for in my life are...

Today, I would **love** to do:

Today **i am focusing** on being...

I AM

I AM

I AM

What did I notice about my **thoughts** today?

What could I have handled **differently** today?

How can I open to **new** possibilities?

What am I **proud** of that came about today?

My Yoga Practice

Meditation   Inspiration

Yoga Practice   ....

6.00

7.00

8.00

9.00

10.00

11.00

12.00

13.00

14.00

15.00

16.00

17.00

18.00

19.00

My Yoga Practice

Meditation   Inspiration

Yoga Practice   ....

6.00

7.00

8.00

9.00

10.00

11.00

12.00

13.00

14.00

15.00

16.00

17.00

18.00

19.00

dream space

date:

gratitude is Wisdom...

Today, I feel **inspired** to do...

I create my day with my **thoughts**, therefore...

I AM

I AM

I AM

What did I **love** about my yoga practice today?

In what ways would I like to **grow**?

What would I like to **let go** of?

What was my underlying **motivation** today?

date:

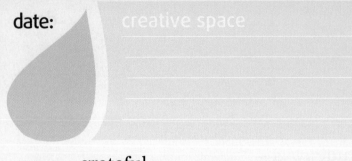

creative space

When I am **grateful** I open up to more...

Meditation   Inspiration

Yoga Practice   ....

What would I do **today**, if it was my last?

6.00

7.00

Today...

I AM

I AM

I AM

8.00

9.00

What was **interesting** about today?

10.00

11.00

12.00

What am I not **seeing**?

13.00

14.00

What ideas would I like to **upgrade**?

15.00

16.00

17.00

When was I completely in the **moment** today?

18.00

19.00

My Yoga Practice

dream space

date:

Today, I give **thanks** for...

■ Meditation　■ Inspiration

■ Yoga Practice　■ ....

My **inspired** actions for today are...

| 6.00 |
| 7.00 |

Today I **honour** how I feel and...

I AM

I AM

I AM

| 8.00 |
| 9.00 |

What was today's **lesson**?

| 10.00 |
| 11.00 |
| 12.00 |

How can I create a more **challenging** yoga practice?

| 13.00 |
| 14.00 |

What do I **know** that I'm not admitting?

| 15.00 |
| 16.00 |
| 17.00 |

What **strengths** did I use today?

| 18.00 |
| 19.00 |

date:

creative space

My Yoga Practice

What I **love** about my work is...

☐ Meditation   ☐ Inspiration

☐ Yoga Practice ☐ ....

Today I am inspired to take these **actions**:

6.00

7.00

I have a **beautiful** mind and...

8.00

I AM

I AM

9.00

I AM

What did I **learn** on the yoga mat today?

10.00

I AM
empowered

11.00

12.00

How was my **mindset** today?

13.00

14.00

What new **habit** do I want to adopt into my life?

15.00

16.00

17.00

Where am I at this very moment?

18.00

19.00

date:

I am so grateful for **simple** things like...

- Meditation
- Inspiration
- Yoga Practice
- ....

What is the best course of **action** to take today?

6.00

7.00

Today I **am** creative and...

8.00

I AM

I AM

9.00

I AM

10.00

Who AM I?

11.00

12.00

What am I supposed to do right **now**?

13.00

14.00

15.00

What new **mindset** do I want to adopt into my life?

16.00

17.00

How did my **yoga** practice feel today?

18.00

19.00

weekly check - in

	09.00	13.00	17.00
	10.00	14.00	18.00
	11.00	15.00	19.00
	12.00	16.00	20.00

What major goals have I achieved this month?

How can I be more congruent with my thoughts, words and actions?

What are the biggest distractions to my yoga practice and how can I remove them?

What is one thing I can do this week that will create the biggest results in my life?

What am I committed to in my life right now?

How can I shine my light more?

What disempowering thoughts are holding me back and how can I upgrade those?

What new pose or asana can I incorporate into my current yoga practice?

- Review Conscious Life Blueprint
- Review Purpose Statement
- Update 90-Day Planner
- Add Actions to Weekly Planner
- Plan Your Week

Old Habit >

New Habit >

New Actions >

New Affirmation/Mantra/Yoga Pose

weekly planner

4 Major Goals I'm Focused On This Week:

1	2	3	4

Projects & Appointments For This Week	Target date	Actions & Yoga Practice For This Week	Target date
monday			
tuesday			
wednesday			
thursday			
friday			
saturday			
sunday			

date:

creative space

Today I am so **grateful** for...

Meditation   Inspiration

Yoga Practice   ....

My top 3 **inspired actions** for today are...

6.00

7.00

My **intentions** for today are...

I AM

I AM   8.00

I AM

9.00

What did I notice about my **yoga** practice today?

10.00

11.00

12.00

What did I **learn** today?

13.00

14.00

After today, what **behaviour** do I want to upgrade?   15.00

16.00

17.00

What **strengths** did I use today?

18.00

          19.00

date:

My Appreciation & gratitude list

Meditation   Inspiration

Yoga Practice   ....

Today, I am most inspired to do...

6.00

7.00

The mindset I wish to create today is...

I AM

I AM

8.00

I AM

9.00

What did I enjoy about today?

10.00

11.00

12.00

What challenged me today that I can learn from?

13.00

14.00

What new yoga pose would I like to perfect?

15.00

16.00

17.00

What did I do really well today?

18.00

19.00

date:

The things I am **grateful** for in my life are...

☐ Meditation   ☐ Inspiration

☐ Yoga Practice   ☐ ....

Today, I would **love** to do:

6.00

7.00

Today **i am focusing** on being...

I AM

I AM

I AM

8.00

9.00

What did I notice about my **thoughts** today?

10.00

11.00

12.00

What could I have handled **differently** today?

13.00

14.00

How can I open to **new** possibilities?

15.00

16.00

17.00

What am I **proud** of that came about today?

18.00

19.00

My Yoga Practice

Meditation Inspiration

Yoga Practice ....

6.00

7.00

8.00

9.00

10.00

11.00

12.00

13.00

14.00

15.00

16.00

17.00

18.00

19.00

dream space date:

gratitude is Wisdom...

Today, I feel inspired to do...

I create my day with my thoughts, therefore...

I AM

I AM

I AM

What did I love about my yoga practice today?

In what ways would I like to grow?

What would I like to let go of?

What was my underlying motivation today?

date:

When I am **grateful** I open up to more...

Meditation   Inspiration

Yoga Practice   ....

What would I do **today**, if it was my last?

6.00

7.00

Today...
I AM
I AM
I AM

8.00

9.00

What was **interesting** about today?

10.00

11.00

12.00

What am I not **seeing**?

13.00

14.00

What ideas would I like to **upgrade**?

15.00

16.00

17.00

When was I completely in the **moment** today?

18.00

19.00

date:

Meditation   Inspiration

Yoga Practice   ·················

6.00

7.00

8.00

9.00

10.00

11.00

12.00

13.00

14.00

15.00

16.00

17.00

18.00

19.00

Today, I give **thanks** for...

My **inspired** actions for today are...

Today I **honour** how I feel and...

I AM

I AM

I AM

What was today's **lesson**?

How can I create a more **challenging** yoga practice?

What do I **know** that I'm not admitting?

What **strengths** did I use today?

weekly check - in

	09.00	13.00	17.00
	10.00	14.00	18.00
	11.00	15.00	19.00
	12.00	16.00	20.00

What have I achieved this week?

What's working with my practice and why is it working?

What's not working and what am I willing to do to upgrade it?

What is one thing I can do this week that will create the biggest results in my life?

What do I need to make a decision about?

How can I be more authentic?

What beliefs are holding me back and how can I upgrade them?

How can I open my chakras for more connection to my source?

☐ Review Conscious Life Blueprint

☐ Review Purpose Statement

☐ Update 90-Day Planner

☐ Add Actions to Weekly Planner

☐ Plan Your Week

Old Habit >

New Habit >

New Actions >

New Affirmation/Mantra/Yoga Pose

weekly planner

4 Major Goals I'm Focused On This Week:

1	2	3	4

Projects & Appointments For This Week	Target date	Actions & Yoga Practice For This Week	Target date
monday			
tuesday			
wednesday			
thursday			
friday			
saturday			
sunday			

date:

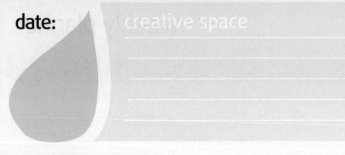

creative space

My Yoga Practice

What I **love** about my work is...

Today I am inspired to take these **actions**:

I have a **beautiful** mind and...

I AM

I AM

I AM

What did I **learn** on the yoga mat today?

How was my **mindset** today?

What new **habit** do I want to adopt into my life?

Where am I at this very moment?

Meditation   Inspiration

Yoga Practice   ....

6.00

7.00

8.00

9.00

10.00

11.00

12.00

13.00

14.00

15.00

16.00

17.00

18.00

19.00

date:

I am so grateful for simple things like...

Meditation Inspiration

Yoga Practice ·················

6.00

7.00

What is the best course of action to take today?

8.00

9.00

10.00

11.00

12.00

13.00

14.00

15.00

16.00

17.00

18.00

19.00

Today I am creative and...

I AM

I AM

I AM

Who AM I?

What am I supposed to do right now?

What new mindset do I want to adopt into my life?

How did my yoga practice feel today?

date:

creative space

My Yoga Practice

Today I am so **grateful** for...

■ Meditation	■ Inspiration
■ Yoga Practice	■ ....

My top 3 **inspired actions** for today are...

6.00

7.00

My **intentions** for today are...

I AM

I AM

I AM

8.00

9.00

What did I notice about my **yoga** practice today?

10.00

11.00

12.00

What did I **learn** today?

13.00

14.00

After today, what **behaviour** do I want to upgrade?

15.00

16.00

17.00

What **strengths** did I use today?

18.00

19.00

dream space

date:

My Appreciation & gratitude list

Meditation	Inspiration
Yoga Practice	....

Today, I am most inspired to do...

6.00

7.00

The mindset I wish to create today is...

8.00

I AM

I AM

9.00

I AM

10.00

What did I enjoy about today?

11.00

12.00

What challenged me today that I can learn from?

13.00

14.00

15.00

What new yoga pose would I like to perfect?

16.00

17.00

What did I do really well today?

18.00

19.00

date:

creative space

The things I am grateful for in my life are...

Today, I would love to do:

Today i am focusing on being...

I AM

I AM

I AM

What did I notice about my thoughts today?

What could I have handled differently today?

How can I open to new possibilities?

What am I proud of that came about today?

Meditation   Inspiration

Yoga Practice   ....

6.00

7.00

8.00

9.00

10.00

11.00

12.00

13.00

14.00

15.00

16.00

17.00

18.00

19.00

dream space

date:

gratitude is Wisdom...

Meditation   Inspiration

Yoga Practice   ....

6.00

7.00

8.00

9.00

10.00

11.00

12.00

13.00

14.00

15.00

16.00

17.00

18.00

19.00

Today, I feel inspired to do...

I create my day with my thoughts, therefore...

I AM

I AM

I AM

What did I love about my yoga practice today?

In what ways would I like to grow?

What would I like to let go of?

What was my underlying motivation today?

weekly check - in

	09.00	13.00	17.00
	10.00	14.00	18.00
	11.00	15.00	19.00
	12.00	16.00	20.00

What projects have I completed this week?

What's going well with my practice and why is it?

What do I find most challenging in my life right now?

What is one thing I can do this week that will create the biggest results in my life?

What am I happy about right now?

How can I be more empowered in my thoughts, words and actions?

What fears are holding me back and how can I overcome those?

How does my body feel? Am I feeling grounded?

Review Conscious Life Blueprint

Review Purpose Statement

Update 90-Day Planner

Add Actions to Weekly Planner

Plan Your Week

Old Habit >

New Habit >

New Actions >

New Affirmation/Mantra/Yoga Pose

weekly planner

4 Major Goals I'm Focused On This Week:

1	2	3	4

Projects & Appointments For This Week	Target date	Actions & Yoga Practice For This Week	Target date
monday			
tuesday			
wednesday			
thursday			
friday			
saturday			
sunday			

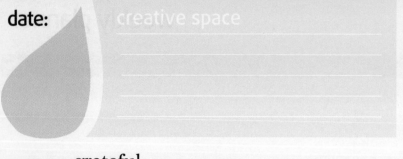

date:

creative space

When I am **grateful** I open up to more...

What would I do **today**, if it was my last?

Today...
I AM
I AM
I AM

What was **interesting** about today?

What am I not **seeing**?

What ideas would I like to **upgrade**?

When was I completely in the **moment** today?

Meditation   Inspiration

Yoga Practice   ....

6.00

7.00

8.00

9.00

10.00

11.00

12.00

13.00

14.00

15.00

16.00

17.00

18.00

19.00

dream space

date:

Meditation

Inspiration

Yoga Practice

....

6.00

7.00

8.00

9.00

10.00

11.00

12.00

13.00

14.00

15.00

16.00

17.00

18.00

19.00

Today, I give **thanks** for...

My **inspired** actions for today are...

Today I **honour** how I feel and...

I AM

I AM

I AM

What was today's **lesson**?

How can I create a more **challenging** yoga practice?

What do I **know** that I'm not admitting?

What **strengths** did I use today?

date:

creative space

What I **love** about my work is...

Today I am inspired to take these **actions**:

I have a **beautiful** mind and...

I AM

I AM

I AM

What did I **learn** on the yoga mat today?

How was my **mindset** today?

What new **habit** do I want to adopt into my life?

Where am I at this very moment?

My Yoga Practice

Meditation   Inspiration

Yoga Practice   ....

6.00

7.00

8.00

9.00

10.00

11.00

12.00

13.00

14.00

15.00

16.00

17.00

18.00

19.00

date:

Meditation   Inspiration

Yoga Practice   ....

6.00

7.00

8.00

9.00

10.00

11.00

12.00

13.00

14.00

15.00

16.00

17.00

18.00

19.00

I am so grateful for **simple** things like...

What is the best course of **action** to take today?

Today I **am** creative and...

I AM

I AM

I AM

Who AM I?

What am I supposed to do right **now**?

What new **mindset** do I want to adopt into my life?

How did my **yoga** practice feel today?

date:

creative space

Today I am so **grateful** for...

My top 3 **inspired actions** for today are...

My **intentions** for today are...

I AM

I AM

I AM

What did I notice about my **yoga** practice today?

What did I **learn** today?

After today, what **behaviour** do I want to upgrade?

What **strengths** did I use today?

Meditation Inspiration

Yoga Practice ....

6.00

7.00

8.00

9.00

10.00

11.00

12.00

13.00

14.00

15.00

16.00

17.00

18.00

19.00

My Yoga Practice

dream space

date:

My Appreciation & gratitude list

Meditation   Inspiration

Yoga Practice   ....

Today, I am most inspired to do...

6.00

7.00

The mindset I wish to create today is...

I AM

I AM

8.00

I AM

9.00

10.00

What did I enjoy about today?

11.00

12.00

What challenged me today that I can learn from?

13.00

14.00

What new yoga pose would I like to perfect?

15.00

16.00

17.00

What did I do really well today?

18.00

19.00

weekly check - in

	09.00	13.00	17.00
	10.00	14.00	18.00
	11.00	15.00	19.00
	12.00	16.00	20.00

What have I achieved on my Conscious Life Blueprint this week?

- Review Conscious Life Blueprint
- Review Purpose Statement
- Update 90-Day Planner
- Add Actions to Weekly Planner
- Plan Your Week

What do I need to start or stop?

In my relationships, how can I communicate better?

Old Habit >

What is one thing I can do this week that will create the biggest results in my life?

New Habit >

What am I proud about right now?

How can I be happier and more grateful?

New Actions >

What negative attitudes are holding me back and how can I overcome those?

New Affirmation/Mantra/Yoga Pose

How can I stretch myself further in my yoga practice?

weekly planner

1　　　　**2**　　　　**3**　　　　**4**

Projects & Appointments For This Week	Target date	Actions & Yoga Practice For This Week	Target date
monday			
tuesday			
wednesday			
thursday			
fr day			
saturday			
sunday			

date:

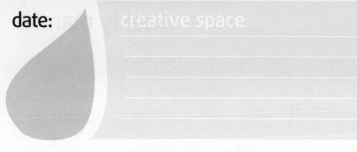

creative space

The things I am **grateful** for in my life are...

Today, I would **love** to do:

Today **i am focusing** on being...

I AM

I AM

I AM

What did I notice about my **thoughts** today?

What could I have handled **differently** today?

How can I open to **new** possibilities?

What am I **proud** of that came about today?

Meditation   Inspiration

Yoga Practice   ....

6.00

7.00

8.00

9.00

10.00

11.00

12.00

13.00

14.00

15.00

16.00

17.00

18.00

19.00

dream space

date:

gratitude is Wisdom...

Meditation   Inspiration

Yoga Practice   ·················

6.00

7.00

8.00

9.00

10.00

11.00

12.00

13.00

14.00

15.00

16.00

17.00

18.00

19.00

Today, I feel **inspired** to do...

I create my day with my **thoughts**, therefore...

I AM

I AM

I AM

What did I **love** about my yoga practice today?

In what ways would I like to **grow**?

What would I like to **let go** of?

What was my underlying **motivation** today?

date:

creative space

When I am **grateful** I open up to more...

Meditation ☐   Inspiration ☐

Yoga Practice ☐   ☐ ....

What would I do **today**, if it was my last?

6.00

7.00

Today...
I AM
I AM
I AM

8.00

9.00

What was **interesting** about today?

10.00

11.00

12.00

What am I not **seeing**?

13.00

14.00

What ideas would I like to **upgrade**?

15.00

16.00

17.00

When was I completely in the **moment** today?

18.00

19.00

My Yoga Practice

dream space

date:

Today, I give **thanks** for...

- Meditation
- Inspiration
- Yoga Practice
- ....

My **inspired** actions for today are...

6.00

7.00

Today I **honour** how I feel and...

I AM

I AM

8.00

I AM

9.00

What was today's **lesson**?

10.00

11.00

12.00

How can I create a more **challenging** yoga practice?

13.00

14.00

I AM connected to my divine essence

15.00

What do I **know** that I'm not admitting?

16.00

17.00

What **strengths** did I use today?

18.00

19.00

date:

creative space

What I **love** about my work is...

Today I am inspired to take these **actions**:

I have a **beautiful** mind and...

I AM

I AM

I AM

What did I **learn** on the yoga mat today?

How was my **mindset** today?

What new **habit** do I want to adopt into my life?

Where am I at this very moment?

Meditation   Inspiration

Yoga Practice   ....

6.00

7.00

8.00

9.00

10.00

11.00

12.00

13.00

14.00

15.00

16.00

17.00

18.00

19.00

dream space

date:

Meditation

Inspiration

Yoga Practice

....

6.00

7.00

8.00

9.00

10.00

11.00

12.00

13.00

14.00

15.00

16.00

17.00

18.00

19.00

I am so grateful for **simple** things like...

What is the best course of **action** to take today?

Today I **am** creative and...

I AM

I AM

I AM

Who AM I?

What am I supposed to do right **now**?

What new **mindset** do I want to adopt into my life?

How did my **yoga** practice feel today?

weekly check - in

	09.00	13.00	17.00
	10.00	14.00	18.00
	11.00	15.00	19.00
	12.00	16.00	20.00

What major goals have I achieved this month?

How can I be more congruent with my thoughts, words and actions?

What are the biggest distractions to my yoga practice and how can I remove them?

What is one thing I can do this week that will create the biggest results in my life?

What am I committed to in my life right now?

How can I shine my light more?

What disempowering thoughts are holding me back and how can I upgrade those?

What new pose or asana can I incorporate into my current yoga practice?

- Review Conscious Life Blueprint
- Review Purpose Statement
- Update 90-Day Planner
- Add Actions to Weekly Planner
- Plan Your Week

Old Habit >

New Habit >

New Actions >

New Affirmation/Mantra/Yoga Pose

weekly planner

| 1 | 2 | 3 | 4 |

Projects & Appointments For This Week	Target date	Actions & Yoga Practice For This Week	Target date
monday			
tuesday			
wednesday			
thursday			
friday			
saturday			
sunday			

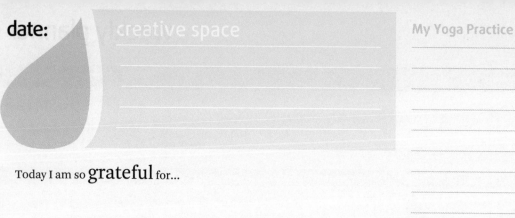

date:

creative space

My Yoga Practice

Today I am so grateful for...

My top 3 **inspired actions** for today are...

	Meditation		Inspiration
	Yoga Practice		....

My **intentions** for today are...

I AM

I AM

I AM

6.00

7.00

What did I notice about my **yoga** practice today?

8.00

9.00

10.00

What did I **learn** today?

11.00

12.00

13.00

After today, what **behaviour** do I want to upgrade?

14.00

15.00

16.00

17.00

What **strengths** did I use today?

18.00

19.00

date:

My Appreciation & gratitude list

Meditation	Inspiration
Yoga Practice	....

Today, I am most inspired to do...

6.00

7.00

8.00

The mindset I wish to create today is...

I AM

I AM

9.00

I AM

10.00

What did I enjoy about today?

11.00

12.00

What challenged me today that I can learn from?

13.00

14.00

15.00

What new yoga pose would I like to perfect?

16.00

17.00

What did I do really well today?

18.00

19.00

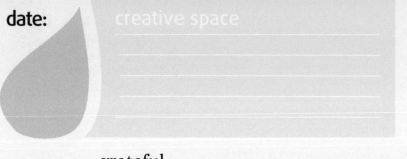

date:

creative space

The things I am **grateful** for in my life are...

Meditation   Inspiration

Yoga Practice   ....

6.00

Today, I would **love** to do:

7.00

Today **i am focusing** on being...

8.00

I AM

I AM

9.00

I AM

What did I notice about my **thoughts** today?

10.00

11.00

12.00

What could I have handled **differently** today?

13.00

14.00

How can I open to **new** possibilities?

15.00

16.00

17.00

What am I **proud** of that came about today?

18.00

19.00

dream space

date:

gratitude is Wisdom...

Meditation

Inspiration

Yoga Practice

. . . .

6.00

7.00

8.00

9.00

10.00

11.00

12.00

13.00

14.00

15.00

16.00

17.00

18.00

19.00

Today, I feel **inspired** to do...

I create my day with my **thoughts**, therefore...

I AM

I AM

I AM

What did I **love** about my yoga practice today?

In what ways would I like to **grow**?

What would I like to **let go** of?

What was my underlying **motivation** today?

date:

creative space

When I am **grateful** I open up to more...

Meditation   Inspiration

Yoga Practice   ....

6.00

7.00

What would I do **today**, if it was my last?

8.00

9.00

Today...
I AM
I AM
I AM

10.00

What was **interesting** about today?

11.00

12.00

13.00

What am I not **seeing**?

14.00

15.00

What ideas would I like to **upgrade**?

16.00

17.00

When was I completely in the **moment** today?

18.00

19.00

date:

Today, I give **thanks** for...

Meditation   Inspiration

Yoga Practice   ·················

My **inspired** actions for today are...

6.00	
7.00	
8.00	
9.00	

Today I **honour** how I feel and...

I AM

I AM

I AM

What was today's **lesson**?

10.00	
11.00	
12.00	
13.00	

How can I create a more **challenging** yoga practice?

14.00	
15.00	

What do I **know** that I'm not admitting?

I AM connected to my divine essence

16.00	
17.00	

What **strengths** did I use today?

18.00	
19.00	

Yearly Review

If you've made it to this point in the journal, you've likely gone through an incredible body-mind transformation! Congratulations on your amazing commitment, discipline and willingness to dive deeper and explore all that life has to offer through yoga, meditation, self-inquiry and the process of personal transformation. Now it's time to reflect back over your year and note your achievements, your lessons, your challenges and your break-throughs, and celebrate how far you've come! Use these observations as stepping stones to catapult you into another beautifully conscious year.

Help us spread our transformational journals with your friends by:

Sharing your journal images using hashtag #dailygreatnessjournal on social media or review the Dailygreatness Yoga Journal on our website or on Amazon and go in our monthly draw to win a free copy!

To reorder your Dailygreatness Yoga Journal and browse all our other journals, online courses and content, visit www.dailygreatnessjournal.com

- ☐ Review your Conscious Life Blueprint

- ☐ Review your Purpose Statement

- ☐ Review your Yearly Planner

- ☐ Celebrate your Achievements!

- ☐ Start dreaming of an exciting new vision for next year

How has my yoga practice improved?

What goals have I achieved?

In what ways has my life changed for the better?

What have I learned about myself?

What have I learned about others?

How am I embracing change?

What new positive habits have I adopted?

What breakthroughs have I had?

What do I need to let go of before moving forward into another year?

What areas of personal growth would I like to explore next year?

What major goals would I like to achieve next year?

What are my yoga inspired goals for next year?

Appendix i

A 6-Step Process for Creating and Achieving Meaningful Goals:

1 Desire & Aspire

Setting your goal. WHAT do you desire to have or aspire to be? This is the biggest picture of what you want to be, do or have in any area of your life. Your goal is the final outcome, not a project or action towards something, but the ultimate goal you are aiming for. What would you love to do, be or achieve? What do you feel passionate about? What have you always wished for? What is deep within your heart waiting to be expressed? Take some time to look within and notice the answers that arise.

2 Purpose

WHY do you want it? A strong why is the motivation you need to propel you towards your goals. If you can't find a big enough why, you may need to re-evaluate and decide if your goal is something you really want. A good question to ask is, "When I achieve this goal will I be happier and have more of what is important to me?"

3 Mindset

WHO do you need to be? This step is all about the mindset behind your goal. If you want to be a successful leader, then you need to be a leader and develop the mindset of someone who is a good leader. If you want to lose weight, then you need to be a healthy person and develop the habits and mindset of a healthy person. If you want to make more money, then you need to be someone who has an abundance mindset. Once you step into BE-ing, then you will DO the actions and you will HAVE the results.

4 Action

HOW will you make it happen? Make a plan by breaking down your goals into smaller projects and your projects into actions. Use the Dailygreatness Yoga Journal goal planners to stay on track and follow up on your goals every day, week and quarter throughout the year.

5 Timeframe

WHEN will you have it? Make a deadline for when you will complete each action, project and goal, but remember you'll need to stay flexible. Hold-ups and unforeseen challenges happen all the time.

6 Self-Awareness

WHICH fears, obstacles or limiting beliefs will you likely come up against? Now is the time to be honest with yourself and get all your fears, limiting beliefs and potential challenges out in the open. By recognising them, you can prepare yourself for when they arrive – and trust me, they will. When you're aware of these challenges, you'll see them for what they are, and by not giving them your power, you can keep moving past them and achieve your goals and realise your dreams.

Appendix ii

Tips for a Mindful Meditation Practice

Sit in a comfortable position. You may like to sit on a chair, or cross-legged on the floor (you can sit on a blanket, towel or book if that helps your knees and hips relax a little more). You want to be able to completely relax while staying fully alert. Close your eyes and begin to focus on your breath.